Communicating with the Public

Also available from Bloomsbury

Discourse and Identity on Facebook, by Mariza Georgalou
Facebook and Conversation Analysis, by Matteo Farina
Language, Identity and Symbolic Culture, edited by David Evans
Searchable Talk, by Michele Zappavigna
The Art of Political Storytelling, by Philip Seargeant

Communicating with the Public

Conversation Analytic Studies

Edited by
Hansun Zhang Waring and
Elizabeth Reddington

BLOOMSBURY ACADEMIC
LONDON • NEW YORK • OXFORD • NEW DELHI • SYDNEY

BLOOMSBURY ACADEMIC
Bloomsbury Publishing Plc
50 Bedford Square, London, WC1B 3DP, UK
1385 Broadway, New York, NY 10018, USA
29 Earlsfort Terrace, Dublin 2, Ireland

BLOOMSBURY, BLOOMSBURY ACADEMIC and the Diana logo are
trademarks of Bloomsbury Publishing Plc

First published in Great Britain 2020
This paperback edition published in 2022

Copyright © Hansun Zhang Waring, Elizabeth Reddington and Contributors, 2020

Hansun Zhang Waring and Elizabeth Reddington have asserted their right under the
Copyright, Designs and Patents Act, 1988, to be identified as Editors of this work.

For legal purposes the Acknowledgments on p. xiv constitute an extension
of this copyright page.

All rights reserved. No part of this publication may be reproduced or transmitted
in any form or by any means, electronic or mechanical, including photocopying,
recording, or any information storage or retrieval system, without prior permission
in writing from the publishers.

Bloomsbury Publishing Plc does not have any control over, or responsibility
for, any third-party websites referred to or in this book. All internet addresses given
in this book were correct at the time of going to press. The author and publisher regret
any inconvenience caused if addresses have changed or sites have ceased to exist,
but can accept no responsibility for any such changes.

A catalogue record for this book is available from the British Library.

A catalog record for this book is available from the Library of Congress.

Library of Congress Control Number: 2020940859

ISBN: HB: 978-1-3500-9818-3
        PB: 978-1-3501-9914-9
        ePDF: 978-1-3500-9819-0
        eBook: 978-1-3500-9820-6

Typeset by Integra Software Services Pvt. Ltd.

To find out more about our authors and books visit www.bloomsbury.com
and sign up for our newsletters.

To the #lansibunch (h.)
For O, with gratitude (E)

Contents

List of Figures	ix
Foreword *John Heritage*	x
Acknowledgments	xiv

Part 1 Overview

1 Introduction *Elizabeth Reddington and Hansun Zhang Waring* — 3

Part 2 Doing Messaging

2 Beyond Neutrality and Adversarialness: The Case of *Platform Questions* Hansun Zhang Waring — 25
3 Enabling Institutional Messaging: TV Journalists' Work with Interviewee Responses *Carol Hoi Yee Lo and Di Yu* — 49
4 Constructing the Audience in Media Interviews *Nadja Tadic and Di Yu* — 67

Part 3 Managing Logistics

5 *But*-prefacing for Refocusing in Public Talk *Ann Tai Choe and Elizabeth Reddington* — 87
6 Curating the Q&A: The Art of Moderating Webinars *Allie Hope King* — 111
7 Narrating the Visual in Webinar Q&As *Di Yu and Nadja Tadic* — 131

Part 4 Negotiating Identities

8 Constructing Expertise: Person Reference in Audience
   Members' Self-Identification in Public Talk Q&A Sessions
   Ignasi Clemente   149
9 Gaze as a Resource for Creating Coherence across Speakers
   during Moderated Panel Discussions *Christopher
   D. Van Booven*   169

Notes on Contributors   188
Index   192

Figures

7.1 Webinar interface   133
7.2 Participant raises hand virtually   133

Foreword

John Heritage
University of California at Los Angeles

Relative to much of what has previously been studied by discourse and conversation analysts, the studies reported in this volume present a new and distinctive world of social phenomena. *Communicating with the Public* is a sustained examination of a diverse set of public relations activities associated with a large non-profit philanthropic medical foundation, pseudonymized here as the Better Living Health Foundation (BLHF). Its authors draw from a common pool of data in which foundation representatives of various kinds conduct webinars to promulgate grant information and discuss measures for public health improvement in panel presentations and public talks. There are also podcast interviews in which foundation representatives interview health experts, and other interviews in which foundation personnel are interviewed in programs for transmission on local television. At the core of these communications is the promotion of the foundation's perspectives on public health and, as part of this, the presentation of the foundation's own expertise, beneficence, and its value and significance to the world of health policy and practice.

There are a lot of moving parts in the foundation's process of self-presentation, and they are implemented through a wide variety of interactional practices that are the subject of these studies. Quite a number of these practices are distinctive, unfamiliar even, to those of us who study task-focused interactions and public communication, and they offer both striking and valuable continuity and contrast with the results of earlier research.

Prior research on public discourse is of two general sorts. First there are meetings, either public or semi-private, that are focused on an agenda. Research on these meetings has tended to focus on the details of their interactional management through relatively formal turn-taking systems. The background here is that meetings with a large number of participants are liable to break down or "schism" into multiple "sidebar" conversations. The very existence of a meeting is threatened by these tendencies, and with it the possibility of achieving meeting goals is also at risk. Standard solutions to these problems involve the role of chairpersons to whom contributions should be directed, and who will allocate next turns among the participants. Public meetings, business meetings, and classrooms among others quite easily fall into this mediated form of turn-taking organization. And this is very present in Allie Hope King's study of webinar moderators who select questioners (or questions) and allocate them to others for response. Significantly, as King notes, even small-scale failures in specific turn-allocation can cause significant problems. Moderators often have the advantage of information that is inaccessible to other participants and this, as Di Yu and Nadja Tadic describe, can create an obligation to "narrate" the visual content of their screens to justify moderating decisions that may be unique to the world of webinars.

In the second kind of public communication that has attracted a large amount of study, the interactants are positioned as antagonists in a public contest. Courtroom interaction is an obvious example of this kind. Here, quite granular rules of conduct organize the ordering and contents of questions, and narrowly restrict participation, all in the interest of fairness among participants. News interview interaction is also quite tightly regulated by tacit rules that prevent explicit disagreement between interviewers and interviewees, and limit conflict among the latter. Underlying, indeed necessitating, these rules are the terms of what Clayman and Heritage termed the "interview contract." The interviewee is interested in promoting a point of view, while interviewers are trying to create engaging news stories that challenge interviewee perspectives while avoiding the attribution of news bias. On the whole, interviewers tend to have a rather low opinion of their interview subjects. In the words of one observer, "The working hypothesis almost universally shared among correspondents is that politicians are suspect; their public images probably false, their public statements disingenuous, their moral pronouncements hypocritical, their motives self-serving, and their promises ephemeral." The fingerprint of this stance is to be found in adversarial questioning that contradicts the interviewee's public pronouncements, undermines their presuppositions, and throws doubt on their motivations. This kind of questioning is noticeably absent from the interview data provided in this volume. Instead, interviewers go out of their way to promote the agendas of interviewees and to showcase their achievements, in ways that somewhat resemble the questioning that Laura Loeb describes as occurring in celebrity chat shows.

In BLHF interviews, as Hansun Waring shows, interviewees are invited to expand on elements of foundation activities that are already framed as praiseworthy. Interviewers may take up an openly naïve stance toward the achievements of BLHF programs, or build questions that serve as springboards for the recitation of BLHF achievements. These essentially supportive actions are just as prominent in the follow-up questions with which, as Carol Lo and Di Yu show, interviewers invite the further elaboration of foundation goals, perspectives, and achievements. It is fascinating to observe the broader institutional frameworks that these alternative interview forms inhabit. In general news production, professional, independently financed journalists interrogate politicians and other public figures in the interests of public accountability. The BLHF interviews were broadcast on local TV stations, and a majority were underwritten by the BLHF itself. Even though the journalist participants had been recipients of Emmy awards for broadcasting, the lines of influence are perhaps not too difficult to discern.

In other chapters, notably those on linguistic practices concerned with basic communicative functions, we see clear continuities with other strands of research on public communication. Identity work by interview participants on television, and by audience members in the question and answer sessions of public meetings, though directed to ends that are particular to the health context, is insightfully analyzed by Nadja Tadic and Di Yu and by Ignasi Clemente respectively. Chapters on the pragmatic functions of *but*-prefaced turns as resource for the redirection of talk (Ann Tai Choe and Elizabeth Reddington), and of gaze as a feature of management among speakers in moderated panel discussions (Christopher Van Booven), also offer fresh insights.

Although the analytic techniques used in these studies will be familiar to discourse and conversation analysts, the empirical contexts of these analyses are very distinctive and their findings not only elucidate forms of institutional communication that may be unfamiliar to many but also force us to reconsider older findings in this new comparative dimension. *Communicating with the Public* illuminates the breadth and complexity of the public relations communications of a well-funded organization, and the multiplicity of the pragmatic resources that enter into its communication processes. In so doing this volume both provides continuity with prior research and shines a bright contrastive light on earlier concepts and findings.

Acknowledgments

This volume came together as a result of a multiyear, grant-funded research project examining one philanthropic organization's communication with external audiences in the public sphere. We are grateful for this organization's support and encouragement. All authors represented in the volume worked closely with the data through transcription and analysis. Early versions of some of the chapters were presented as part of the colloquium *Communicating with the Public: "Third Parties" in Question-Answer Sequences,* organized by Hansun Zhang Waring for the 2018 Georgetown University Round Table (GURT) in Washington, D.C. The works-in-progress benefited greatly from the feedback of the audience members who attended, including John Heritage. Written versions of some of the talks subsequently appeared in an edited forum in *Studies in Applied Linguistics & TESOL* (SALT) at Teachers College, Columbia University. We are also grateful to attendees of *The Language and Social Interaction Working Group* (LANSI) data sessions for their insights at early stages of analysis.

Part One

Overview

1

Introduction

Elizabeth Reddington and Hansun Zhang Waring
Teachers College, Columbia University

The title phrase of this volume, "communicating with the public," may call to mind politicians delivering speeches to crowds or journalists interviewing prominent figures on national news programs—events that have been the subject of much scholarly attention (e.g., Atkinson, 1984; Clayman & Heritage, 2002). Yet it could be said that much of the work of communicating with the public occurs outside the national spotlight and without a script. In other words, communicating with the public also involves the routine tasks that an organization's representatives undertake as they participate in a variety of planned events in which they interact with external audiences. Picture, for example, an organization's vice-president taking part in a panel discussion at an industry conference, or a program representative fielding questions during a webinar for prospective applicants. These relatively lower-profile events are nonetheless vital to maintaining an organization's image and promoting its goals, and the interactional maneuvering required to manage them is no less complex for all parties involved.

In this volume, we offer a collection of case studies investigating these complexities, focusing on the efforts of one non-profit organization, a U.S.-based philanthropic foundation, to communicate its mission of improving public health. Examining a diverse array of organized events, including panel discussions, webinars, and television and podcast interviews, these studies reveal how both foundation representatives and their interlocutors target messaging to audiences that may or may not be (physically) present, manage the logistics of delivering this messaging, and position themselves as credible experts or an institutional collective.

The studies in this volume are linked not only by their focus on communication platforms used by a single organization but also by a shared analytic interest and method. Rather than attempting to measure the effectiveness of particular campaign messaging, our interest lies in what might be considered more "mundane" but no less important matters: how an organization's representatives and their interlocutors communicate in the relatively spontaneous interactions that take place during events held *in public* and/or designed for distribution *to the public*. To address this question of *how*, all studies employ conversation analysis (CA), a method that aims to uncover patterns in social interaction through close analysis of participants' use of meaning-making resources, including talk, gaze, gesture, and bodily movement (see *Description of methodology*, this chapter, for a detailed introduction). One of the strengths of CA lies in its attention to interactional practices that speakers routinely engage in but may not be consciously aware of or able to articulate. Focusing on the *how* of communication in this way, not only the *what* (i.e., message content), has the potential to offer a nuanced perspective on the day-to-day work of public relations (see Heath, 2013), contribute to expanding knowledge of non-profit communication in particular (see Koschmann, Isbell, & Sanders, 2015, for a review), and suggest practical recommendations for public-facing representatives of organizations. After all, as Clayman and Heritage (2002) point out with regard to one well-studied form of public communication, the broadcast news interview: "No topic, theme, or perspective can find its way [in] … except through the vehicle of an interactional move by one of the participants" (p. 14). The same may be said of the informational interviews, panel discussions, and question-answer sessions (Q&As) that are our focus and that, to date, have received less attention from scholars.

While these events are diverse in terms of format and participants, it is worth noting that the "unscripted" segments in which we are interested are similarly organized at an interactional level: They are centered around exchanges of questions and responses. Certain participants in each event are afforded the right to ask questions and others the right to respond. Compared to everyday talk, in which participants may take up any conversational role or move at any time, such a system is noticeably more formal and constrained. Of particular interest, then, is how foundation representatives and individuals representing external audiences work within this system, in real time, to engage one another and get their messages across.

In the following sections of this introduction, we first discuss relevant literature on questioning and responding in public settings to better set the current project in context before attempting further specification of our focus on "communicating with the public." Then, we provide a detailed account of the data utilized in the studies and CA methodology. Finally, we offer a brief overview of the studies in the volume and suggest ways in which their findings may be of use to both scholars and practitioners.

Background: Questioning and Responding in Public Settings

Much empirical work on naturally occurring interaction has been devoted to describing the design of questions, the actions they accomplish, and the kinds of responses they mobilize. It is well recognized that utterances produced as questions can do more than seek information; they often serve as "vehicles" for accomplishing other actions (Ford, 2010), such as requesting, offering, or challenging (Hayano, 2013). How participants ask and respond to questions in various kinds of "institutional" encounters has been the subject of significant scholarly attention (Drew & Heritage, 1992; Freed & Ehrlich, 2010; Heritage & Clayman, 2010). A defining feature of many such encounters is interactional asymmetry: It is often the institutional representative or "professional" who asks the questions while the "layperson" or "client" is limited to responding; as a result, the institutional representative maintains greater control over the course of the interaction, over what gets talked about and what gets done (Drew & Heritage, 1992). Close analysis of these encounters has revealed how questioning and responding practices are responsive to participants' orientations to institutional agendas and tasks. In annual medical checkups, for example, doctors have been shown to design their history-taking questions to elicit confirmations of positive states from patients in order to move visits along (Boyd & Heritage, 2006; Heritage, 2010), while in acute care visits, their questions presuppose the existence of a problem (Stivers, 2007; see Hayano, 2013, for further examples). In the courtroom, attorneys engaged in cross-examination routinely use follow-up questions to advance their client's interests. By reformulating key aspects of prior responses in subsequent questions, they work to commit the witness to their own client's version of events (Atkinson & Drew, 1979).

Most relevant to the topic of this volume are investigations of questioning and responding in "public" settings. In the courtroom, for instance, attorney and witness may address questions and responses to each other, but they do so in the presence of a number of other, ratified participants. This "overhearing audience" (Goffman, 1981) consists of the judge and the jury for whom the talk is actually produced (Heritage & Clayman, 2010). That courtroom talk is designed for and directed to this audience can be seen in various interactional patterns and practices. For example, attorneys routinely do not produce receipt tokens, such as *oh* or *yeah*, in response to answers from witnesses. By *not* using such tokens, which are a common feature of question-answer exchanges in everyday conversation, attorneys avoid positioning themselves as primary recipients; they thus display their understanding that information is elicited for the benefit of the overhearing others (Heritage, 1985; Heritage & Clayman, 2010).

Another context in which question-answer exchanges are shaped by participants' orientation to an overhearing audience is broadcast programming (Heritage, 1985; Hutchby, 2005). In the case of such programming, a "live" studio audience may or may not be present during the recording of the interaction, but there is always an "absent" audience of listeners/viewers; the latter may be thought of as "distributed recipients" of the talk, in both the physical and temporal sense (Hutchby, 2005). Perhaps the most well-studied form of broadcast programming is the television and radio news interview (e.g., Blum-Kulka, 1983; Clayman, 2001, 2002, 2007; Clayman & Fox, 2017; Clayman & Heritage, 2002; Harris, 1991; Heritage, 1985; Hutchby, 2005). In more and less explicit ways, journalists position themselves as "tribune of the people," speaking for the broadcast audience or the general public by raising the issues of concern to them (Clayman, 2002, 2007; Clayman & Heritage, 2002). Like attorneys engaged in courtroom questioning, journalists conducting interviews with politicians and other public figures typically avoid producing receipt tokens, treating the audience as the primary recipients of interviewee responses (Clayman & Heritage, 2002; Heritage, 1985). Clayman and Heritage (2002) have shown in detail how journalists use variations in the design of their questions to balance the potentially competing demands of holding interviewees accountable on behalf of the public while maintaining a neutral stance. The public figures being interviewed, for their part, may engage in the practice of "operating" on a question in order to appear cooperative while nevertheless pursuing a shift in the question's agenda (Clayman, 2001).

While the "accountability" interview (Montgomery, 2010) has received significant attention, scholars have also taken an interactional approach to the study of other types of broadcast programming, revealing similarities with and differences from this genre. Television talk shows and radio call-in shows, for instance, can involve a wider range of participant types, including the media professionals who serve as hosts and mediate discussion, "experts" on the topic of the program, and "lay" audience members who may themselves be able to participate directly in the interaction (Thornborrow, 2010). Examining television talk shows, Thornborrow (2001, 2010) has shown how hosts use questions to elicit their guests' opinions on a topic but refrain from evaluation themselves, an action thus reserved for the audience. However, unlike journalists in traditional news interviews, they also use their follow-up turns to dramatize aspects of guests' prior turns for the benefit of the audience. In radio call-in shows centered on advice-giving, Hutchby (2005) has observed that the invited experts orient not only to the caller/questioner in their responses but also to the overhearing audience. Accordingly, answers often come in two parts, with the first part addressed more directly to the caller's question, and the latter providing additional information that may be relevant to a wider audience, thus balancing the tension between the "private" and "public" nature of the advice-giving (Hutchby, 2005, p. 104).

An important feature of the broadcast formats just discussed is the opportunity for direct audience participation. Some scholars have begun to examine the practices of "lay" participants, that is, participants who are not journalists, hosts, public figures, or invited experts, in these and other interactional arenas (Clayman, 2004). For instance, Thornborrow (2010) has shown how talk show audience members produce complex questioning turns that build toward expressing a stance on the topic at hand, managing to address both the host who mediates discussion and the wider audience. Considering the context of town hall meetings, in which "ordinary" citizens interact with politicians, Clayman (2004) has observed that citizen questioners often foreground a personal connection to the topic, a practice that journalists traditionally avoid. Llewellyn (2005) focused on the conduct of citizens taking part in public meetings with local officials and found that audience members worked collaboratively to accomplish such actions as pursuing a response to a question or furthering a complaint.

As this brief review has shown, there has been recurrent interest in examining how, in question-answer exchanges conducted in public settings, participants design their talk in ways that are sensitive to the context and reflect an orientation to a wider audience that may or may not be (physically) present. Much attention has been devoted to the interaction of journalists and public figures; however, less attention has been devoted to other types of interviews that are common in today's broadcast programming, such as interviews with experts on topics of public/social relevance and with private citizens who have some connection to a newsworthy, perhaps local, event or topic (Clayman, 2013; Montgomery, 2010). Montgomery (2010) has argued for distinguishing the "accountability" interview, explored in the work of Clayman and Heritage (2002), from other types of interviews, such as the "experiential" interview, in which "ordinary people" are called on to share experiences and emotions relevant to a topic of wider interest. Indeed, Montgomery (2010) has suggested that the function of these interviews is to give shape to public sentiment and has documented some distinct features of this genre, including a tendency for interviewers to eschew neutrality and strongly affiliate with interviewees. Other public settings in which private citizens engage with institutional representatives have not been widely studied, such as panel discussions and conference Q&A sessions. Organized events in which interaction is enabled and mediated by a technological platform, such as webinars, have also received less attention. The current volume seeks to address these gaps by examining the organization of and the practices characteristic of interaction in such contexts.

It is also worth noting that prior work has often reflected a rather clear distinction between the social categories of professional/expert and layperson, and between the interactional roles of questioner and recipient, with professionals/experts often retaining the power to ask the questions (see also Hutchby, 2005). However, when public-facing representatives of an organization interact, for instance, with potential stakeholders and collaborators, who may themselves be professionals/experts in other/related areas, as is often the case in our dataset, applying social categories in a top-down manner becomes problematic. The question becomes if and how these identities become relevant in real-time interaction. In addition, in many of the events in our dataset, it is members of the audience who question the institution's representatives, and thus wield power to shape the institution's responses. Identifying resources available not only to those with a professional obligation to speak on behalf of an audience (i.e., journalists) but to audience members themselves is a path worth pursuing.

We believe that an examination of such questions and issues will be of interest not only to scholars seeking a deeper understanding of social interaction or public relations but to practitioners as well. As Clayman (2004) observes, in interaction-based informational programming of various kinds, there is "a premium on the ability to speak without a script, deal with unforeseen contingencies, and manage the delicate balancing act of being properly responsive to others while continuing to 'stay on message'" (p. 45). By foregrounding the interactional and contextual demands and challenges inherent in communicating in public and for the public, we hope to offer some practically oriented suggestions, particularly for the institutional representatives who must take on such roles as presenter, moderator, interviewer, or interviewee as part of their work.

Communicating with the Public

As noted above, the current volume examines unscripted interaction within a range of planned communications events. What unites these distinct event types or genres is a special feature of their multiparty structure: Speakers address their interlocutor(s) but do so in a public setting, in the (physical or virtual) presence of, or for the benefit of, an overhearing audience. It is this feature that we hope to capture in the phrase "communicating with the public." We recognize that organizations are advised to plan and target their messaging with more narrowly defined "publics" in mind (Bowen & Rawlins, 2013), yet at the same time, an organization cannot predict exactly who will attend or view/listen to an event. Thus, we have chosen to use the singular and general term, "the public," a catch-all for the co-present parties and potential future audiences for these events, connected by a shared interest (professional and/or personal) in the topic of health and one organization's work related to that topic.

"Communicating with the public" can be viewed as an interactional "problem" or challenge not only for an organization's representatives who, broadly put, seek to engage with individuals not currently affiliated with or informed about the organization and its mission. We also consider it an interactional problem for the interviewers and audience members who question those representatives. Notably, in contexts such as Q&A sessions following conference or webinar talks, who is a "speaker" and who is "the audience" can shift from moment to moment. As a result, this volume includes work that addresses practices utilized by such parties. In one way or another, the studies thus aim to address the question: How do participants with various affiliations, agendas, and interactional roles communicate in and/or for the public?

Description of Data

All chapters in this book draw from a common corpus of data, which consists of a variety of publicly available audio- and video-recordings of events that involve representatives of the Better Living Health Foundation (pseudonym) communicating their mission and programs (e.g., Framework for Health— also a pseudonym) devoted to improving public health to external audiences (i.e., audiences outside the foundation). These recordings include twenty-five webinars, ten moderated panel presentations and discussions, and eight public talks, all of which end with Q&A sessions that many of our chapters focus on. Briefly, webinars provide a forum for foundation representatives to deliver program information to potential grant applicants and answer questions about those programs, whereas in panel presentations and discussions as well as public talks given at universities and conferences, foundation representatives discuss issues related to improving public health in front of a live audience. The recordings also include nine podcast interviews, where experts are interviewed by foundation representatives, and six televised interviews, where foundation representatives are interviewed on local news programs to publicize their work. The recorded events took place over a three-year period (2014–2017).

The participants across the various forums are presenters (identified in transcript excerpts as *PR*), panelists (PA), moderators (MO), audience members (AU), interviewers (IR), interviewees (IE), and, in one particular case, an automated voice (AT). Presenters typically include not only foundation officers but also individuals from other non-profit organizations, government agencies, or academic institutions who may be grantees or working in partnership with the foundation in advancing its mission. As such, all presenters represent the foundation's interests to various extents and are referred to as "foundation representatives" in the chapters. More detailed descriptions of the data as relevant to the focus of each study can be found in the individual chapters. Note that all references to specific people, organizations, and places have been anonymized.

All interviews as well as the Q&A portions of the other events have been transcribed in their entirety using the following standard conversation analytic notations (Jefferson, 2004) along with some modifications to capture the timing of nonverbal conduct:

.	(period) falling intonation.
?	(question mark) rising intonation.
,	(comma) continuing intonation.
-	(hyphen) abrupt cut-off.
::	(colon(s)) prolonging of sound.
word	(underlining) stress.
word	the more underlining, the greater the stress.
WORD	(all caps) loud speech.
°word°	(degree symbols) quiet speech.
↑word	(upward arrow) raised pitch.
↓word	(downward arrow) lowered pitch.
>word<	(more than and less than) quicker speech.
<word>	(less than and more than) slowed speech.
<	(less than) jump start or rushed start.
hh	(series of h's) aspiration or laughter.
.hh	(h's preceded by period) inhalation.

(hh)	(h's in parentheses) inside word boundaries.
[ ] [ ]	(lined-up brackets) beginning and ending of simultaneous or overlapping speech.
=	(equal sign) latch or contiguous utterances of the same speaker.
(2.4)	(number in parentheses) length of a silence in tenths of a second.
(.)	(period in parentheses) micro-pause, 0.2 second or less.
( )	(empty parentheses) non-transcribable segment of talk.
(syl syl)	number of syllables hearable in non-transcribable talk.
((*gazing toward S*))	(double parentheses) non-speech activity or transcriptionist comment, italicized.
{((*words*))-words}	dash to indicate co-occurrence of nonverbal behavior and verbal elements; curly brackets to mark the beginning and ending of such co-occurrence if necessary.
(try 1)/(try 2)	(two parentheses separated by a slash) alternative hearings.
$word$	(dollar signs) smiley voice.
#word#	(number signs) creaky voice.
rt	right, as in *raises rt hand*
lt	left, as in *raises lt hand*

As can be seen, these notations capture not just what is said, but also when (e.g., whether in overlap with another's talk or gesture or after a period of silence) and how something is said—with what volume, pitch, speed, voice quality, and the like. When it comes to nonverbal conduct, in the case of ((*directs gaze and points to PA3*))-exter<u>nality</u> argument, for example, the dash indicates that the speaker utters "externality argument" *at the same time* as he gazes at and points to PA3. Finally, the absence of the dash would suggest that the gaze and pointing occur *prior to* the utterance.

Description of Methodology

Unifying the chapters in this book is not only a common corpus of data but also a singular method of analysis—that of CA or "the science of analyzing conversations second by second," as social scientist Elizabeth Stokoe (2014) describes it in her TED talk. As a form of "naturalistic inquiry" (Schegloff, 1997, p. 501), CA insists on using data collected from naturally occurring interaction as opposed to interviews, field notes, native intuitions, and experimental methodologies (Heritage, 1984, p. 236). Analysts work with audio- or video-recordings along with the transcripts of these recordings, using transcription notations that capture a full range of interactional details (see above). The goal of CA is to uncover the tacit methods and procedures of social interaction. Analysis begins with the meticulous inspection of single instances and is guided by the question, "Why that now?" (Schegloff & Sacks, 1973), that is, why is a particular bit of talk produced in that particular format at that particular time? What is it accomplishing? It is through such close interrogation of the data that we find evidence of participants' own methods of accomplishing particular "actions," for example, how moderators do the work of moderating, how interviewers support the messaging of interviewees, and how panelists enact being a team. Although decades of conversation analytic research have successfully generated crucial insights into the professional competencies in a wide range of institutional contexts (e.g., Antaki, 2011; Drew & Heritage, 1992; Sarangi & Roberts, 1999), CA as an analytical tool has not yet, to our knowledge, been applied to what we see as a new domain of inquiry—that of communicating with the public in the specific context of institutional representatives interacting with external audiences in public.

As any other methodology, CA comes with its own set of foundational concepts or analytical tools. We briefly introduce here a few of these terms that will be repeatedly encountered across the chapters (Sacks, Schegloff, & Jefferson, 1974; Schegloff, 2007; Schegloff, Sacks, & Jefferson, 1977):

- **Turn-constructional unit (TCU)** is a unit out of which and by reference to which speakers set out to fashion a turn. A TCU carries the feature of **projectability**; that is, the possible completion of the TCU can be projected, whether it is a word, a phrase, a clause, or a sentence. **Possible**

completion point (PCP)** is the possible end of a TCU. Except for cases where, for example, a multi-unit turn as in a story is in progress, the possible completion of a TCU also makes transition to a next speaker relevant. In that case, PCP is also the **transition-relevance place (TRP)**.
- At teach transition-relevance place, a set of **turn-allocation** "rules" apply and apply in quick succession: (a) **current selects next**. (b) If not (a), next speaker **self-selects**. (c) If not (b), **current speaker continues**, and (a) and (b) repeat.
- **Sequence** is a course of action implemented through talk (e.g., a request sequence can consist of a request and its granting/rejection).
- **Adjacency pair (AP)** is a basic unit of a sequence, which consists of a sequence of two turns produced by different speakers and ordered as **first-pair part (FPP)** and **second-pair part (SPP)**. Upon the production of a first-pair part, a second pair-part is **made conditionally relevant** (e.g., an invitation makes conditionally relevant acceptance or rejection).
- **Preference** is an organization in which the alternatives that fit in a certain slot in talk (e.g., second-pair parts in an adjacency pair) are treated as nonequivalent. Some are **preferred**; others are **dispreferred**. Preferred actions are "seen but unnoticed." They are the "natural," "normal," and "expected" actions. Their absence is noticeable. The absence of the preferred response is a basis for inferring the presence of the dispreferred response. For example, after an invitation, acceptance is preferred and refusal dispreferred. The absence of acceptance is the basis for inferring refusal. Preferred actions are typically produced without delay, mitigation, or accounts, and dispreferred actions *with* such features.
- **Repair** is an organization for addressing problems in speaking, hearing, and understanding. Repair of a **trouble source** can be initiated by "self" (the trouble-source speaker) or "other" and completed by self or other, engendering such varying trajectories as **self-initiated self-repair, self-initiated other-repair, other-initiated self-repair**, and **other-initiated other-repair**.

Before we move on, it may be worth noting that gold-standard measures for sound research such as validity, reliability, and generalizability take on special meanings when it comes to judging the credibility of CA research. To consider validity in CA is to think about whether the analysis produced by the researcher is in fact uncovering participants' practices of social interaction or "measuring" what it is supposed to "measure." Ensuring validity then involves obtaining high-quality recordings, producing detailed transcripts that accurately represent the recordings, and, finally, demonstrating empirically defensible analyses with publicly available transcripts against which the readers can make their independent judgments with regard to the tenability of the analysis. In other words, the transparency of analytical claims grounded in specific participant conduct is an important validation procedure in CA. These same measures are also integral to ensuring the reliability of CA findings. Given that the transcripts (and ideally recordings) are subject to repeated scrutiny by multiple readers, to ensure that the same data would yield consistent analyses across time and individuals, analysts not only engage in repeated close analyses on their own but also routinely attend data sessions, where participants hold each other accountable for the analyses they produce *vis-à-vis* a particular transcript along with its audio-/video-recordings—a process that discourages open-ended "reading into" the transcripts or recordings. Finally, the familiar notion of generalizing from a sample to a population is ill-suited to a CA study, which produces what is *possible* in other settings, not what is generalizable in the sense of "the traditional 'distributional' understanding of generalizability" (Peräkylä, 2004, pp. 296–297). Put otherwise, what CA research produces, as Pomerantz (1990) points out, is analytical generalization (Yin, 2003), where each case is related to a "theory" (p. 233). That is, by analyzing individual instances, the machinery which produced these individual instances is revealed (Benson & Hughes, 1991, pp. 130–131). Each instance is evidence that "the machinery for its production is culturally available, involves members' competencies, and is therefore possibly (and probably) reproducible" (Psathas, 1995, p. 50).

Overview of the Chapters

The remaining chapters of this book are organized into three broad sections that highlight the types of actions various participants accomplish in the context of communicating with the public: doing messaging (Part II), managing logistics (Part III), and negotiating identities (Part IV).

Drawing exclusively from the interview data that involve mostly public television interviewers and representatives of the Better Living Health Foundation, all three chapters in Part II on doing messaging delve into the specific ways in which the interviewers and interviewees promote the visibility, enhance the accessibility, or calibrate the target of institutional messaging. In Chapter 2, Waring describes three types of *platform questions* built by the interviewers (IRs) for the interviewees (IEs) to "glow and shine": (1) *yes/no* questions that feign confusion, (2) *wh*-questions that presuppose a laudable quality of the IE or the institution, and (3) invitations to elaborate preceded by a positive formulation of the IE's background or the institution's reputation. In Chapter 3, instead of focusing on IR questions, Lo and Yu examine how interviewers follow up on interviewee responses. In particular, they show how in these follow-up turns, the interviewers facilitate the interviewees' messaging on behalf of their institution by either (1) providing additional information to contextualize or clarify IE responses or (2) reformulating IE talk to make foundation messaging concrete for the audience. Finally, in Chapter 4, Tadic and Yu shift their analytical spotlight toward the interviewees themselves and show how, through specific linguistic choices, the interviewees display expectations of who their audience members are, what knowledge and experiences they possess, and what their goals and values might be.

If Part II may be construed as addressing the "content" of institutional messaging, Part III on managing logistics showcases a collection of chapters addressed to such matters during interviews, panel discussions, and informational webinars as digressions, technical difficulties, asymmetrical visual access, and any threats to the smooth transition between audience questions and panelist answers. In Chapter 5, Choe and Reddington show how the discourse marker *but* functions as a refocusing device that helps a speaker shift from talk that departs from the objective at hand to pursue the original course of action, thereby regaining the focus of discussion for the benefit of the overhearing audience (Goffman, 1981). The next two chapters focus on moderator conduct during informational webinars. In Chapter 6, King shows how moderators, in an effort to ensure smooth transitioning between audience questions and panelist answers during voice-only webinars, use *question preliminaries* and *question animation* in presenting questions and *respondent selection* in managing responses. Also focusing on moderator conduct, Yu and Tadic in Chapter 7 describe the practice of *narrating the visual*, which is engaged by moderators to remediate the problem of asymmetrical visual access during webinars, and, more specifically, to: (1) prospectively account for and project an upcoming action such as closing or initiating a sequence, (2) retrospectively account for a prior delay and signal to the audience that the event is still ongoing, or (3) simultaneously account for a prior interactional issue and a forthcoming interactional project.

In Part IV on negotiating identities, we shift the focus from doing messaging and managing logistics toward the work participants engage in to situate who they are in the institutional events of public talks and moderated panel discussions. Analyzing data from Q&A sessions of public talks, Clemente in Chapter 8 shows how audience members self-identify by using the formulation of *first and last name + affiliation* to establish themselves as institutional representatives whose identity is relevant to the nature of the question and whose personal involvement and work furnish support for how they come to know what they know. Finally, rather than focus on audience identities, Van Booven in Chapter 9 makes evident how panelists during moderated panel discussions engage the method of *tacit embedded addressing* through gaze shifts to accomplish the seemingly irreconcilable task of speaking as individuals while being heard as a multi-person collectivity.

Intended Audience of the Book

For students and scholars in applied linguistics and communication studies, and especially those with a conversation analytic interest in institutional discourse, this book unveils the uncharted territory of "communicating with the public." Within this new terrain, topics of perennial interest such as the question-answer sequence are revisited with new insights, and a plethora of previously undocumented interactional practices such as *platform questions* or *narrating the visual* make their analytic debut.

For practitioners charged with the task of communicating with the public in fields such as public relations, public health, and journalism, we hope that the collective findings of this volume will constitute usable knowledge for enhancing training and improving practices. Such knowledge, as will be shown in the ensuing chapters, entails how to ask and answer questions in ways that facilitate and crystalize institutional messages (Chapters 2–3); how to navigate such practical challenges as digressions, technical difficulties, and asymmetrical visual access in virtual interaction (Chapters 5–7); and, finally, how to speak as a panelist or ask questions "as a professional" (Chapters 8–9). Importantly, and perhaps surprisingly for many practitioners, this inventory of "how's" is a far cry from simple bullet-point directives (e.g., "stay on message") and can only be located in the fine-grained details of social interaction, where even subtle language choices can have a big impact (e.g., *but*-prefaced utterances to refocus digressive talk or pronoun choices that include or exclude a particular segment of the audience). We hope that practitioners who read this book will be inspired to notice patterns in the seeming "messiness" of unscripted talk, and, ultimately, become analysts of their own (developing) expertise in their continuing pursuit of specifying and implementing best practices.

References

Antaki, C. (Ed.). (2011). *Applied conversation analysis: Intervention and change in institutional talk*. Basingstoke: Palgrave Macmillan.

Atkinson, J. M. (1984). *Our masters' voices: The language and body language of politics*. London: Methuen.

Atkinson, J. M., & Drew, P. (1979). *Order in court*. London: Macmillan.

Benson, D., & Hughes, J. (1991). Method: Evidence and inference for ethnomethodology. In G. Button (Ed.), *Ethnomethodology and the human sciences* (pp. 109–136). Cambridge: Cambridge University Press.

Blum-Kulka, S. (1983). The dynamics of political interviews. *Text*, 3(2), 131–153.

Bowen, S. A., & Rawlins, B. L. (2013). Publics. In R. L. Heath (Ed.), *Encyclopedia of public relations* (pp. 761–762). Thousand Oaks, CA: Sage.

Boyd, E., & Heritage, J. (2006). Taking the history: Questioning during comprehensive history taking. In J. Heritage & D. W. Maynard (Eds.), *Communication in medical care: Interaction between primary care physicians and patients* (pp. 151–184). Cambridge: Cambridge University Press.

Clayman, S. E. (2001). Answers and evasions. *Language in Society*, 30(3), 403–442.

Clayman, S. E. (2002). Tribune of the people: Maintaining the legitimacy of aggressive journalism. *Media, Culture & Society*, 24(2), 197–216.

Clayman, S. E. (2004). Arenas of interaction in the mediated public sphere. *Poetics*, *32*, 29–49.
Clayman, S. E. (2007). Speaking on behalf of the public in broadcast news interviews. In E. Holt & R. Clift (Eds.), *Reporting talk: Reported speech in interaction* (pp. 221–243). Cambridge: Cambridge University Press.
Clayman, S. E. (2013). Conversation analysis in the news interview. In J. Sidnell & T. Stivers (Eds.), *The handbook of conversation analysis* (pp. 630–656). Malden, MA: Blackwell Publishing.
Clayman, S. E., & Fox, M. P. (2017). Hardballs and softballs: Modulating adversarialness in journalistic questioning. *Journal of Language and Politics*, *16*(1), 20–40.
Clayman, S. E., & Heritage, J. (2002). *The news interview: Journalists and public figures on the air*. Cambridge: Cambridge University Press.
Drew, P., & Heritage, J. (Eds.). (1992). *Talk at work: Interaction in institutional settings*. Cambridge: Cambridge University Press.
Ford, C. (2010). Questioning in meetings: Participation and positioning. In A. F. Freed & S. Ehrlich (Eds.), *"Why do you ask?" The function of questions in institutional discourse* (pp. 211–234). Oxford & New York: Oxford University Press.
Freed, A. F., & Ehrlich, S. (Eds.). (2010). *"Why do you ask?" The function of questions in institutional discourse*. Oxford & New York: Oxford University Press.
Goffman, E. (1981). *Forms of talk*. Philadelphia, PA: University of Pennsylvania Press.
Harris, S. (1991). Evasive action: How politicians respond to questions in political interviews. In P. Scannell (Ed.), *Broadcast talk* (pp. 76–99). London: Sage.
Hayano, K. (2013). Question design in conversation. In J. Sidnell & T. Stivers (Eds.), *The handbook of conversation analysis* (pp. 395–414). Oxford & New York: Wiley-Blackwell.
Heath, R. L. (Ed.). (2013). *Encyclopedia of public relations* (Vols. 1–2). Thousand Oaks, CA: Sage.
Heritage, J. (1984). *Garfinkel and ethnomethodology*. Oxford: Basil Blackwell.
Heritage, J. (1985). Analyzing news interviews: Aspects of the production of talk for an overhearing audience. In T. A. Van Dijk (Ed.), *Handbook of discourse analysis* (Vol. 3) (pp. 95–119). New York: Academic Press.
Heritage, J. (2010). Questioning in medicine. In A. F. Freed & S. Ehrlich (Eds.), *"Why do you ask?" The function of questions in institutional discourse* (pp. 42–68). Oxford & New York: Oxford University Press.
Heritage, J., & Clayman, S. E. (2010). *Talk in action: Interactions, identities, and institutions*. Malden, MA: Wiley-Blackwell.

Hutchby, I. (2005). *Media talk: Conversation analysis and the study of broadcasting*. New York: McGraw-Hill Education.

Jefferson, G. (2004). Glossary of transcript symbols with an introduction. In G. Lerner (Ed.), *Conversation analysis: Studies from the first generation* (pp. 13–31). Amsterdam: John Benjamins.

Koschmann, M. A., Isbell, M. G., & Sanders, M. L. (2015). Connecting nonprofit and communication scholarship: A review of key issues and a meta-theoretical framework for future research. *Review of Communication, 15*(3), 200–220.

Llewellyn, N. (2005). Audience participation in political discourse: A study of public meetings. *Sociology, 39*(4), 697–714.

Montgomery, M. (2010). Rituals of personal experience in television news interviews. *Discourse & Communication, 4*(2), 185–211.

Peräkylä, A. (2004). Reliability and validity in research based on naturally occurring social interaction. In D. Silverman (Ed.), *Qualitative research: Theory, method, and practice* (2nd ed.) (pp. 283–304). London: Sage.

Pomerantz, A. (1990). On the validity and generalizability of conversation analytic methods: Conversation analytic claims. *Communication Monographs, 57*(3), 231–235.

Psathas, G. (1995). *Conversation analysis: The study of talk-in-interaction*. Thousand Oaks, CA: Sage.

Sacks, H., Schegloff, E. A., & Jefferson, G. (1974). A simplest systematics for the organization of turn-taking for conversation. *Language, 50*(4), 696–735.

Sarangi, S., & Roberts, C. (Eds.). (1999). *Talk, work and institutional order: Discourse in medical, mediation and management settings*. New York: Mouton de Gruyter.

Schegloff, E. A. (1997). Practices and actions: Boundary cases of other-initiated repair. *Discourse Processes, 23*(3), 499–545.

Schegloff, E. A. (2007). *Sequence organization in interaction: A primer in conversation analysis* (Vol. 1). Cambridge: Cambridge University Press.

Schegloff, E. A., & Sacks, H. (1973). Opening up closings. *Semiotica, 7*, 289–327.

Schegloff, E. A., Jefferson, G., & Sacks, H. (1977). The preference for self-correction in the organization of repair in conversation. *Language, 53*(2), 361–382.

Stivers, T. (2007). *Prescribing under pressure: Parent-physician conversations and antibiotics*. London: Oxford University Press.

Stokoe, E. (2014). The Conversation Analytic Role-play Method (CARM): A method for training communication skills as an alternative to simulated role-play. *Research on Language and Social Interaction, 47*(3), 255–265.

Thornborrow, J. (2001). Questions, control, and the organization of talk in calls to a radio phone-in. *Discourse Studies, 3*(1), 119–143.

Thornborrow, J. (2010). Questions and institutionality in public participation broadcasting. In A. F. Freed & S. Ehrlich (Eds.), *"Why do you ask?" The function of questions in institutional discourse* (pp. 279–296). Oxford & New York: Oxford University Press.

Yin, R. K. (2003). *Case study research: Design and methods* (3rd ed.). London: Sage.

Part Two

Doing Messaging

2

Beyond Neutrality and Adversarialness: The Case of *Platform Questions*

Hansun Zhang Waring
Teachers College, Columbia University

Introduction

Scholars in language and social interaction have offered illuminating accounts of how questions are deployed to accomplish various institutional tasks (e.g., Clayman & Heritage, 2002; Freed & Ehrlich, 2010; Tracy & Robles, 2009). Beyond their obvious utility to seek information, questions have been shown to convey information (Koshik, 2010), communicate identity and relationships (Heritage & Clayman, 2010; Raymond, 2010), reassure or affiliate (Hepburn & Potter, 2010), pursue views and test commitments (Speer, 2010), exercise control in workplaces (Holmes & Chiles, 2010), embody participation and positioning in meetings (Ford, 2010), incriminate (Sidnell, 2010), and nail down a suspect in police interviews (Stokoe & Edwards, 2010).

Conversation analytic research on news interviews, in particular, has produced revealing insights into their institutional features. Much has revolved around interviewers' (IRs) questioning practices in Anglo-American society that embody such competing journalistic norms as neutrality and adversarialness (Heritage & Clayman, 2002) as journalists are expected to maintain objectivity as they seek truth for the public on the one hand and hold public figures accountable on behalf of the public on the other. One way to maintain the fiction of neutrality while engaging in adversarial questioning, for example, is for journalists to speak on behalf of a third party, be it experts in specific knowledge domains or the public. In addition, because questioning is "conventionally understood as a neutralistic action," journalists work hard to "package their actions as 'questions'" (Heritage & Clayman, 2002, p. 6). In fact, much can be packaged into the question to assert pressure on the interviewees by setting the agenda, building in presuppositions, and designing preferences to facilitate one type of answer over another. Clayman and Fox (2017) also show how interviewers can modulate the degree of adversarialness, yielding various kinds of softball or hardball questions. While *what*-questions tend to deliver softballs "with supportive grounds that are weak or nonexistent" (e.g., *The prosecution says you're a con man, a thief ... What's your response to that?*), *how*-questions are built as hardballs where "the tone of pessimism contributes to the sense that the viewpoint is compelling and difficult to counter" (e.g., *One of the criticisms ... How do you answer that?*) (Clayman & Fox, 2017, pp. 30–32). Finally, Clayman and Loeb (2018) demonstrate how journalists use what they call "political positioning questions" to maintain an adversarial stance as they seek confirmation on the recipient's potentially problematic position, seek comments on others' positions that are incongruent with those of the recipient, or propose a mainstream position that is at odds with the recipient's.

One type of TV interview where the IR questioning practices may fall outside the bounds of neutrality and adversarialness concerns programming designed to promote the interviewees (IEs) and/or the missions and agendas of their institutions. In this particular context, the interviewers appear to be charged with a different sort of task—one that supports the IEs' communication with the public, often on behalf of the institution. In this chapter, I show how this particular task is accomplished interactionally via the deployment of what I call *platform questions*.

Data

Data come from four one-on-one interviews (IN1–IN4) that involve two interviewers (IRs) and four interviewees (IEs) on two local television stations (A and B) in different states in the United States. The interviews appear on four different programs, three of which (from Station A) (IN1–IN3) are devoted to: (1) examining the state's public policy issues; (2) featuring public figures (e.g., political leaders, CEOs, television personalities, professors, artists, and educational innovators) and their accomplishments; and (3) tackling state-centric issues including finances, business, education, family, healthcare, and technology. It is worthy of note that the programming on which these interviews appear is underwritten by the foundation the interviewees represent. The fourth interview (IN4) (from Station B) appears on a local news program. The Station-A interviewer (IR1) for the first three interviews (IN1–IN3) is an Emmy-award-winning broadcaster and host of the three programs devoted to the state's public affairs. The Station-B interviewer (IR2) for the fourth interview (IN4) is also an Emmy-award-winning journalist and anchor of the news program on which the interview appears. The interviewees for the first three programs are representatives of the foundation, and the interviewee for the fourth interview is a medical expert who has been working for the station and is about to assume a leadership role at the foundation. Each interview lasts approximately ten minutes, and the questions and answers revolve around the foundation's mission to promote public health and/or the interviewee's work dedicated to that mission.

For the purpose of this chapter, following Ehrlich and Freed (2010), I define questions as any piece of talk designed to create a slot for responding by soliciting (or that is treated as soliciting) information, confirmation, or action (p. 6) (e.g., *Talk about it.*). An initial analysis of the four interviews yielded a small collection of the sixteen platform questions that constitute the basis of this study. Although one would expect the interviewer to be "friendly" across the four interviews given either the interviewee's status as a longtime colleague (Station B) or the foundation's role as a supporter of the programming (Station A), all sixteen "pure" platform questions appear in the first three interviews (IN1–IN3) from Station A. In order to delineate the boundary of these practices, I first show what the *non*-platform questions from the dataset look like. In the segment below, for example, the interviewee is bringing his description of the foundation's initiative to a close (lines 01–02), and the interviewer's two *wh*-questions (*how long* and *when*) (lines 03–04) are designed to fact-check the timeline of the initiative without ostensibly promoting the initiative itself:

(1) IN2 how long
```
01   IE:         in this one community. so that's really exciting.
02               one- basically one: neighborhood.
03   IR:    →    how long is this going for (.) an' when're you
04               gonna look at it >in terms of< say hey, how
05               successful have we been with this.
06   IE:         yeah so the first step of this program is- what
07               we're gonna do ((continues))
```

It is worth noting that any question may be responded to in a way that promotes the answerer's own agenda (Clayman, 2001; Lee, 2013; Stivers & Heritage, 2001), which is a possibility the answerer in the above extract may be pursuing. My focus, however, is on questions, not answers, that do such promoting.

Aside from neutral, information-seeking questions, another type of *non-platform* question is of a more (however subtly) challenging nature. The next segment is taken from the fourth interview, where (as noted earlier) the interviewee is a longtime colleague at Station B and the incoming president of the foundation. The segment begins with him finishing describing the foundation's initiative in lines 01–03:

(2) IN4 how would you

```
01   IE:         hh it's something that everyone
02               has an opportunity a fair opportunity
03               to be healthy.
04   IR:   →     but how would you as the head of the foundation,
05   IE:         yeah.
06   IR:         uh: affect people not being able to afford, more
07               expensive fruits and vegetables. [ it's  ] more
08   IE:                                          [right.]
09   IR:         expensive than potatoes,
10   IE:         right.
11   IR:         or pasta,
12   IE:         yeah.
13   IR:   →     uh::: and how will you- how can you do- how
14               can- how can you as a- the head of the foundation,
15               affect that.
16   IE:         [well you know I-]
17   IR:         [ >you're talking ] about
18               [huge social economic change.<]
19   IE:         [   I    have    a      lot     ]
20               to learn. ((continues))
```

Note that the interviewer's question in line 04 begins with a *but*, foreshadowing some sort of contrast with what the interviewee has just said. Indeed, compared to the grandiose messaging of *everyone has a fair opportunity to be healthy* (lines 01–03), the IR's *how* question places that messaging within the specificity of *fruits and vegetables ... or pasta* (lines 07 and 11). He then proceeds to make a direct connection between the interviewee's new position as *head of the foundation* and the ability of *people* to afford fruits and vegetables (lines 13–15). By uncharacteristically attributing the responsibility for providing such "mundane" items as fruits and vegetables to the highest-ranking position of a foundation, the IR's question, one might argue, is hearable as a challenge of some sort. The "challenging" nature of the question is also evidenced in his ensuing quick-paced comment *you're talking about huge social economic change* (lines 17–18), which treats the issue of providing fruits and vegetables as not easily accomplishable, but a problem with serious complexities. In addition, the question appears to be treated as a challenge by the interviewee, who begins his response with a *well* that suggests the non-straightforward nature of his answer to come (Schegloff & Lerner, 2009) (line 16) and the syntactically optional item *you know* (Clayman & Raymond, 2015) that further delays the response, and this somewhat "choppy" turn beginning is followed by the admission that he does not yet have all the answers (lines 19–20), constituting further support for the argument that the question is treated as challenging by the interviewee as well. In sum, neither the information-seeking questions nor the challenging questions as shown above constitute the focus of this chapter.

Analysis and Findings

As will be shown, unlike neutral questions that simply seek information or challenging questions that demand accountability for the interviewees' claims, *platform questions* are designed as "platforms" for the IEs to "glow and shine," and, as such, are built in three different formats: (1) invite IE to elaborate upon the laudable (e.g., *you have an impressive background in ... tell us what X means.*); (2) feign naivety to amplify the laudable (e.g., *and that's health?*); and (3) steer IE talk toward the laudable (e.g., *so Better Living Health Foundation decides to do what.*). In various ways, these questions create a space for the interviewees to credibly broadcast core missions of the institution in ways that highlight their unique and distinctive features.

Invite IE to Elaborate upon the Laudable

Of the sixteen cases in the "platform questions" collection, seven are built in the format of *invitation to elaborate upon the laudable*. The following three extracts have been chosen from two different interviews to showcase the different ways this format may materialize in actual interaction. Extract 3 is taken from the beginning of IN1, where the interviewer launches immediately into his first question in line 02. As noted earlier, for the purpose of this chapter, a question is defined, following Ehrlich and Freed (2010), as any piece of talk designed to create a slot for responding by soliciting (or is treated as soliciting) information, confirmation, or action. The IR's *talk to us about the foundation* creates such a slot for responding.

(3) IN1 real impact
```
01   IE:         it's great to be here, Joe.
02   IR:    →    .hh talk to us about the foundation.=I mean
03                people hear about the Better Living Health
04                Foundation and its uh its si:ze? its impact, but
05                not a lot of people know (.) uh the real impact.=
06                [talk ] about it.
07   IE:         [mm.]
08                .hh well. .hh we're a foundation that's (.) as you
09                kno:w the largest foundation devoted solely to:
10                improving health and healthcare in this country.
11                .hh but what (.) we're really excited about right now
12                is a vision ((lines omitted)) and that is what we're
13                making our north star (.) at the foundation.
```

Notably, the interviewer does not stop after the first turn-constructional unit (TCU) (Sacks, Schegloff, & Jefferson, 1974) that has sufficiently made a response relevant. Rather, without leaving any space for such a response, he employs latching to launch the next TCU that begins with *I mean*, which appears to set the stage for providing some background for the question— that the foundation is known (*people hear about* X) for *its size* and *its impact* (lines 02–05). This is done before the interviewer redoes his original question with the anaphoric *it* (*talk about it*) (line 06), which refers back to the foundation's *real impact* that *not a lot of people know* (lines 04–05). He has, in other words, moved from *talk to us about the foundation* in more general terms to the more targeted *talk to us about the foundation's real impact*. Put otherwise, the response slot is now refashioned to only accommodate a positive report from the interviewee.

Thus, two moves have been made to construct the "platform" for the interviewee response before that response is produced. The foundation that the IE represents has been cast in a positive light with regard to its reputation, and the initial question has been recalibrated to now explicitly invite the interviewee to expand upon a laudable quality of the foundation (i.e., its *real impact*).

That the platform question is also treated by the interviewee as an opportunity to "glow and shine" is seen in her response that begins with a confirming *mm* in line 07 and continues with affirmation of the size of the foundation (*largest*) and its core mission (*devoted solely to ...*) (lines 09–10). More importantly, she also takes the opportunity to publicize the foundation's new vision (*but what we're really excited about right now*) (lines 11–12). In the end, she does not actually talk about the *real impact* sought by the interviewer but does, however, take advantage of the platform set up by the question to advance her own agenda as the foundation's representative.

The invitation to elaborate is not always launched in such direct terms as *talk about X* and may take more than one turn to execute. The following segment begins with the interviewee's description of the foundation's current mission, and as she brings that account to a close in line 06, the interviewer offers *the other thing* that the foundation is *very actively engaged in* (lines 07–08). By mentioning *these local health rankings* without any explication or asserting partial knowledge of what the foundation does, the interviewer's assertion may be heard as an invitation to respond (i.e., a question) (Heritage, 2012; Labov & Fanshel, 1977; Pomerantz, 1980).

(4) IN3 actively engaged
```
01    IE:         hh an' that we're having
02                not only .h uhm physical health and mental
03                well-being, .h but that we also have communities
04                that are healthy in terms of their economic
05                vibrancy, .h that they have safe places for
06                people to live and to be physically active.
```

```
07   IR:    →    the other thing the uhm Better Living Health
08                Foundation is very actively engaged in is these
09                local health rankings.
10   IE:           mhm,
11   IR:    →    these are health rankings around the relative
12                health of the people and the- the twenty one
13                counties of Anystate?
14   IE:           yeah. .hh so the local health rankings we've
15                been doing it for six years with our partners at
16                University of Anystate, .h .tch we rank ((continues))
```

Note that built into this initial rather implicit question is also a rather implicit positive attribution. First, *local health rankings* is introduced as *the other thing* that the foundation does in addition to all the laudable endeavors that the IE has been describing, such as ensuring *safe places for people to live and to be physically active* (lines 05–06). In other words, *local health rankings* is yet another laudable endeavor. Second, the phrasing of *actively engaged* further creates the image of the foundation being a diligent and dedicated leader in advancing a good cause.

However, this platform to "shine" is not immediately taken up by the interviewee. As can be seen, the IR's implicit invitation to respond is only met with a continuer *mhm* (line 10) that seems to simply acknowledge that *local health rankings* is indeed what the foundation is actively engaged in. Having failed to secure any explication from the IE, the interviewer proceeds to provide that explication himself, ending in a rising intonation that seeks confirmation (lines 11–13). It is in response to this second assertion of recipient-related activities coupled with the rising intonation that the IE steps onto the "platform" to further amplify what has by now been presented as a laudable effort. Thus, the platform question in this extract develops across turns, where the initial minimal assertion of X with its embedded positive attribution is followed up with a brief explication of X that invites confirmation.

Finally, the interviewer's invitation to elaborate can be built upon the IE's own report on some laudable activities that the foundation (which the IE represents) has been engaged in. The following segment begins with the IE's response to the IR's question of what the foundation does to help a third party, Dr. Spark, and his work—by connecting him to others *who can tell the story* (line 05):

(5) IN1 supporters of public broadcasting

```
01    IE:            ((lines omitted)) the (.) most important thing
02                   that we did was to connect him with (.) people
03                   like you:? and others [around] the country=
04    IR:                                  [mm.   ]
05    IE:            =.h who can tell the story. because if you .hh
06                   uh are doing great work in one place and no one
07                   knows about it? it's not gonna [spark. ]
08    IR:    →                                     [(why)-] talk
09                   about that because the public awareness part
10                   of this is huge because you are supporters of
11                   public broadcasting,=>have been for a long
12                   time.< why is it so important for the foundation
13                   to help the public to better understand complex
14                   public policy issues, medical issues, healthcare.
15    IE:            .hh we:: in this country have as a (.)
16                   fundamental part of our (.) democracy. .hh
17                   people understanding (.) the problems and
18                   how to solve those problems. .hh so we've
19                   always felt at the foundation that we had a
20                   .hh central uh obligation to: find out what
21                   works? and then to communicate that.=and to
22                   communicate it in ways that people can
23                   understand. and often that means (.) bringing
24                   the data into real life stories that speak to people.
25                   .hh Dr. Spark's work does that so
26                   beautifully. because ((continues))
```

In line 05, the IE begins to provide an account for the "connecting" work that the foundation does, and before that account reaches its completion, the IR begins speaking in transitional overlap (Jefferson, 1983). What gets absorbed in the overlap is a possible *why*-question, which comes to a cutoff as the IR restarts in the clear with the invitation to *talk about that* (lines 08–09). Without a pitch drop after *that*, however, the IR continues with an account of his own that reformulates the IE's report so far as reflecting the foundation's institutional identity as *supporters of public broadcasting* (lines 10–11). In so doing, he solidifies the laudable and "prepares the stage" for the interviewee, so to speak. Still, the IE is not given the floor to respond at this point. What comes next is hearable as an insertion brought off by the latched and rushed delivery of *have been for a long time* (lines 11–12). This inserted "aside" not only upgrades the laudability of the institutional identity but also projects a "return" to the main business, that is, IR questioning. What the interviewer does return to, notably, is not a simple repetition of the earlier *talk about that* but an elaborately built *wh*-question that presupposes the laudable activities (i.e., *help the public to better understand complex public policy issues, medical issues, healthcare*) bound to the category (Sacks, 1992) of *supporter of public broadcasting* established so far (lines 12–14). What the IE is invited to elaborate upon then is the laudable belief (*why is it so important*) that goes hand in hand with these laudable activities. As can be seen, that is exactly what the IE takes it upon herself to explicate—first the foundation's *central obligation* that *we've always felt ... that we had* (lines 18–20) and then the actual work that implements that obligation as exemplified in Dr. Spark's activities (lines 25–26).

In this section, I have examined three cases of platform questions where the interviewee is invited to expand upon a positive attribution (i.e., a laudable X). The format of the invitation varies according to whether it stands alone or is parasitic upon the IE's prior talk, and whether it is built in the form of a syntactic question, an imperative, an assertion (in rising intonation), or a combination of sorts. The positive attribution is also variably positioned as an inserted formulation (e.g., *we have all heard about ...*), an embedded compliment (e.g., *actively engaged in*), or a reformulation of IE talk (e.g., *you're supporters of public broadcasting*). Implemented either in a single turn or across turns, none of the platform questions described so far are completed in a single TCU. This multipart packaging allows the IR to fine-tune the focus of the question, adjust the size of the response slot, and manage the contingencies of the recipient uptake, all aiming toward building the optimal platform for IEs to promote their agendas on behalf of their institutions.

Voice Naivety to Spotlight the Laudable

We now turn to cases (five out of sixteen in the collection) where the interviewer achieves the same goal of building a platform for the IE to "glow and shine" but does so not by ostensibly inviting elaboration on the "laudable," but by voicing (on behalf of the audience) a certain naivety (or even skepticism) with regard to the foundation's mission. In Extract 6 below, the IR calls attention to the mission that the foundation has been promoting and dealing with (lines 01–05, 07 and 09):

(6) IN2 what is it

```
01   IR:       an' the Framework for Health is uh: uh we
02             should talk about it as being led by Better
03             Living Health Foundation .h a:nd I would say
04             full disclosure you're underwriting programming,
05             .h on our partners- [for part]ners at AnystateTV=
06   IE:                          [°mhm°]
07   IR:       =[ and  ] for us as well. promoting, and dealing=
08   IE:        [°right°.]
09   IR        =with this Framework for Health.
10       →     what I:S it and why is it important.=
11   IE:       =mm. I think the Framework for Health is a
12             ↑logical, .h next step where the foundation ha:s
13             bee:n driving towards. ((lines omitted))
14             how do we create these opportunities
15             e- equal opportunities for all individuals to:
16             .hh make choices and take oppor↑tunities an-
17             an' change how they ↑live [so  ] they live
18   IR:                                 [mm]
19   IE:       healthier lives.
```

Up until line 09, there is no clear indication that the IR is treating the foundation mission he has just introduced as inherently laudable in any way. The questioning that begins in line 10, however, does more "platform building" work. By delivering *is* in louder volume with elongation, the otherwise simple and straightforward *wh*-question that seeks a definition of X is now hearable as treating X as not patently accessible, filled with intrigue, and somewhat mysterious, thereby drawing attention to the X that the IE is given the platform to explicate. In addition, with the ensuing *and*-prefaced *why*-question that presupposes X's importance, the IE is afforded an extra answer slot to go beyond his initial explication of X to elaborate upon its importance—affordances that the IE takes full advantage of (not fully shown). Suffice it to say that it quickly becomes clear that X is indeed a laudable mission as it strives for *equal opportunities for all individuals* (line 15) with the ultimate goal of achieving *healthier lives* for everyone (line 19). One might argue that the articulation of this laudable could have been enabled by unmarked *wh*-questions as well, and I believe that is true. By voicing naivety through the questions, however, the laudable is amplified under the spotlight. It is this extra stance marking via the prosodic dramatization of *is*, for example, that turns an otherwise regular question into a platform question.

Unlike the prior case where the interviewer introduces an X for subsequent naive questioning, the interviewer in the next two cases simply voices naivety by treating the interviewee's prior talk as somehow "hard to believe." The extract below begins with the IE's explanation of the foundation's mission, beginning with a description of how people typically think of health (line 02):

(7) IN3 that's health?
```
01   IE:            mhm. .h so building a Framework for Health
02                  a lot of times people think about health as,
03                  whether or not I have health insurance, and
04                  whether or not I can get quality health care
05                  when I need it. when I'm sick. or when
06                  >someone in my family is.< .hh those are
07                  important pieces, but that's not all that goes
08                  into how healthy we are. .hh think about it,
09                  you know, do you have safe places that you
10                  can be physically active, and that you can .hh uh
11                  take your kids out on a ↑walk or ↑play in your
12                  ↑sidewalks. [.hh ]
13   IR:   →                   [that's] health?
14   IE:            do you- ↓that's health. how else do you exercise
15                  if you don't have a community that you can
16                  go out into ((continues))
```

In line 07, the IE launches into a *but*-prefaced shift from the typical thinking about what health is toward how that taken-for-granted conceptualization is not sufficient (*but that's not all that goes into how healthy we are*) (lines 07–08). She then invites the IR (and presumably the television audience) to *think about* if one has access to *safe places* for various activities (lines 08–12), thus suggesting that the latter is also an indicator of *how healthy we are*. This leap from healthcare/insurance to safe places in conceptualizing health is arguably a "drastic" one. Note that in illustrating her *safe places* point, the IE appears to be building a three-part list (Jefferson, 1990) (e.g., *be physically active, take kids out to walk and play, and …*) that continues to line 13.

As such, the IR's question *that's health?* delivered in transitional overlap (Jefferson, 1983) in line 13 may be heard as "early" and thereby interruptive of IE's larger project of her three-part list. At the same time, one might argue, it also promptly voices on behalf of the audience any confusion or skepticism that the conceptual leap from *health insurance* to *safety* might have incurred. It does so by seeking confirmation of what the IE has clearly treated as part of *health* so far. This is reminiscent of the reverse polarity questions (RPQs) identified by Koshik (2002)—a type of *yes/no* question used by teachers to convey reverse polarity assertions in second-language writing conferences (e.g., *Is that background?* meaning *That's not background.*).

In response, the IE comes to a cutoff in line 14 and offers a full-clause repetition of *that's health* rather than a simple confirming "yes." Heritage and Raymond (2012) show how repetitional responses to *yes/no* questions are more agentive than acquiescent compared to simple *yes*-confirmations. In this particular case, we similarly hear agency in IE's repetitional response as she claims ownership of the confirmation *that's health*, with the lowered pitch on *that*, in particular, signaling confirmation despite possible expectations to the contrary. The ensuing account in the form of a *how else*-question then further establishes, in a somewhat challenging tone, the connection between safety and health by reiterating the earlier stated linkage (lines 09–10) between *exercise* and places where one can exercise (lines 14–16).

Thus, the IR's *that's health?* serves to highlight the foundation's novel vision of health via the dramatic move of stopping the IE in her tracks with a *yes/no* question that conveys incredulity. The question also enables the IE's subsequent agentive confirmation along with a reaffirming account that further specifies the novel connection between safety and health. In this case, the novel vision is the laudable that obtains the spotlight via both the questioning and the answering—another case of a dedicated platform duly exploited.

A similar case may be found in the final extract of this section taken from the same interview, where the IE is explaining the foundation's particular approach to health that involves *bringing together* different pieces (lines 01–11 and 13):

(8) IN3 holistic

```
01   IE:      [ mhm. .hh ] yeah having a good paying job makes
02            a difference. .hh income is how we can afford to send
03            our kids to good schools, uh ((lines omitted))
04            .hh hm and also arou:nd education ((lines omitted))
05            .h so all of these things are tied together it really is
06            .h a holistic uh- bringing together of a:ll the things
07            that go into whether or not we're healthy
08            ((lines omitted)) if their kids are healthy
09            >they're gonna be< more focused on the job,
10            be more productive, .h and the healthcare costs
11            for businesses are gonna be lower. [ so] all of
12   IR:                                         [.hh]
13   IE:      those things come together.=
14   IR: →    =that's the so called ((air quotes))-holistic
15            approach?
16   IE:      .hh
17   IR:      to health care?
18   IE:      yeah I mean it's the: I think it's thinking about
19            all of the things that go into our health and
20            really shifting our mindset ((continues))
```

In line 12, at the same time the IE is bringing her response to a close with a *so*-prefaced summative statement, the IR gears up to speak with an inbreath, waits for the completion of the IE's TCU, and launches an un-inverted *yes/no* question that seeks confirmation of the approach as *holistic*—a word used by the IE herself back in line 06. Similar to what we have observed in the prior segment, the mere act of seeking confirmation of what seems to have been clearly stated treats the IE's talk so far as not patently straightforward and warranting some processing on the part of the recipient, or, perhaps more precisely, the overhearing audience.

Note also that given the completion of the IE's answer by line 13, line 14 is a sequential slot in which the IR could have moved on to his next question. By pointing backward with the anaphoric *that* and repeating the IE's term *holistic*, the IR does a re-take and re-packaging of what the IE has described so far as *the holistic approach*, thus reifying via the nominalization, along with the air quotes, the foundation's laudable vision. With this reification, the IE is offered an opportunity—a platform—to further promote the foundation's vision.

As shown, she begins with an inbreath in line 16 and continues after the IR's increment in line 17, where the confirming *yeah* is followed by an elaboration prefaced with *I mean*. It is in this elaboration that we hear the IE's editorialization of the foundation's vision as *shifting our mindset*—a promotional tagline in part made possible by the IR's platform question.

In sum, the platform questions examined in this section share the commonality of voicing a "naive" stance on behalf of the overhearing audience. In performing this "naïve" stance, the interviewer treats the foundation's vision (introduced either by himself or the IE) as not easily comprehensible or expresses skepticism toward it via questioning. Such dramatization effectively spotlights the innovative quality of the laudable and provides a "savoring" space (Tannen, 2007) for IEs to further their promotional agendas. Unlike the cases in the prior section where the laudable is placed on display before a question is launched to invite elaboration, the laudable in the three just-discussed cases is activated via the questioning itself for more focused and heightened publicizing.

Steer IE Talk toward the (To-be-explicated) Laudable

In other cases where the laudable cannot be clearly located prior to the questioning, the interviewer takes the initiative to steer the IE talk toward the laudable via the platform question. Only four out of the sixteen cases in the collection fall into this category. In the first example below, the interviewer is observed to be launching a shift from "just talk" to laudable efforts through his question. The segment begins with the interviewee explaining the foundation's vision:

(9) IN1 not just talk
```
01    IE:         ((lines omitted)) it's creating the opportunity
02                so that every day, uh all day we have the
03                opportunity to make healthy choices.
04    IR:         >but y'know what's interesting< ((lines omitted))
05                people talk about doing those things. but the
06                foundation ((faces camera))-in full disclosure
07        →       ((lines omitted)) but (.) ((points to IE))- the the fact
08                everything you(h) just talked about, isn't something
```

09		you just talk about [from] a public policy point of-=
10	IE:	[mm.]
11	IR	=point of view. .hh the foundation supports
12		efforts to <u>do</u> those things.=<u>talk</u> about
13		some of those efforts.=
14	IE:	=.hh well. .hh we were just talking about (.)
15		what it would take to create a healthy
16		environment for kids in schools. you can go to
17		Anycity now. a:nd see that ((*continues*))

Upon the completion of the IE's turn explaining the foundation's vision in line 03, the interviewer begins his turn with a *but*-preface—the first indication of a shift to come, where *you know what's interesting* functions almost like a story preface that projects a multi-unit turn (line 04). He then appears to start establishing a contrast between what *people* talk about and what the foundation does (lines 05–06). In roughly characterizing what the IE has explained so far as *those things* that the generic *people talk about*, the interviewer treats the foundation's vision to create opportunities for everyone to make healthy choices (lines 01–03) as somewhat unremarkable—in contrast to the actions that the foundation takes beyond talk, as shown in the subsequent lines. This shift to the laudable then becomes the basis for the IR's subsequent platform question *talk about some of those efforts* (lines 12–13). Similar to those cases where the IE invites elaboration on the laudable, here the interviewer also invites elaboration after having stated the laudable (which the IE takes full advantage of, as shown in lines 15–16), except that in this case, the laudable is parasitic upon and triggered by the IE's prior talk.

The shift toward the laudable may also be accomplished more subtly within a much tighter sequential space. In the following segment from IN2, the interviewee's description of a challenge (lines 01–05) becomes fodder for the IR's question in lines 06–07:

(10) IN2 decides to do what

01	IE:	((*lines omitted*)) you saw (it in) Anycity<
02		all these kids that were: .h really challenged to
03		kind of just >you know< pick a <u>pa:th</u> that was
04		gonna lead them to >this healthy constructive
05		adulthood<. .h uhm that we really <u>w</u>ant for kids.

```
06    IR:    →         .h .tch and so the Better Living Health Foundation
07                     (.) decides to do wh̲at. °[let's] talk about this.°
08    IE:                                    [.hh]
09                     yeah so the foundation is really kinda- really
10                     l̲eaned into this idea of how do we: think abou:t
11                     health in ways that involve, not just the absence
12                     of ill- illness but it really the kind of the
13                     opportunity to get healthy and this is s̲uch an
14                     exciting idea because ((continues))
```

As soon as the IE brings his turn to a completion in line 05, we hear the IR's *.h .tch*—pre-beginnings that signal his readiness to talk. The ensuing *and so* builds what is coming up (i.e., the *wh*-question) as a logical extension of what the IE just said. We might also note that the *wh*-question is markedly un-inverted (as opposed to *what does the Better Living Health Foundation decide to do*), which minimizes any disruption to the logical flow an unmarked *wh*-question might incur. As such, the IR is heard as simply facilitating the next bit of the IE's telling that might already be underway while launching a subtle shift from a mere description of a problem to the foundation's laudable role in solving that problem.

The "logical flow" conveyed through "*problem (IE) + and so the foundation decides to do what (IR)*" arguably signals and strengthens the foundation's stature as the "default" problem solver, thereby enhancing its leadership image in the relevant domain. At the same time, by simply assuming that the foundation has made a decision to do something (*decides to do*), the question further positions this particular problem solver as decisive, hands-on, and committed to real work that can make a real difference. In other words, a great deal of positive attribution is built into the IR's question in its particular sequential position. Also note that this is not the end of the IR's questioning package. Without leaving any space for the IE to respond, he launches into the next TCU *let's talk about this* (line 07), with *this* anaphorically referring back to *so … decides to do what*. While the un-inverted *wh*-question seeks a type-specific answer that could in principle be given in a simple phrase, *talk about it* opens up the response slot to a much wider terrain where the laudable can be not just identified, but "talked about" at some length. In so doing, one might argue, the IR is building a wider platform for the respondent (and his institution) to "glow and shine."

As shown, the initial *wh*-question appears to have been taken up immediately as the IE gears up to speak with the inbreath in line 08—in transitional overlap (Jefferson, 1983) with the IR's next TCU (line 07). He then withholds talk until after the IR's *let's talk about this* before launching into a multi-unit turn (lines 09–14) that further broadcasts and explicates the foundation's initiative.

In short, both platform questions described in this section embody a shift from the relatively "mundane" IE talk so far toward the laudable, for which the IE is offered the stage to further publicize. The two questions vary in the amount of space each takes (i.e., multi-unit turn vs. a single TCU) and the degree to which the laudable is made explicit (e.g., *you don't just talk* vs. *and the foundation decides to do what?*).

Discussion and Conclusion

In this chapter, I have shown three different ways in which the interviewer designs his questions as a platform for the interviewee to "glow and shine." He does so by inviting the interviewee to elaborate upon a stated laudable (e.g., *you're supporters of public broadcasting … why is it so important …*), activating the laudable through naïve questioning (*that's health?*), and steering the interviewee's talk toward the to-be-explicated laudable (e.g., *and the foundation decides to do what.*). The larger goal for this particular questioning practice appears to be getting the interviewee to talk about some sort of laudable in support of the interviewee's self-presentation on behalf of the institution that they represent. The key interactional challenge for the interviewer then is to find that laudable to be topicalized via questioning. Sometimes the laudable is simply part of the prepared questions (e.g., *talk about your impact.*). Even outside prepared questions, however, the interviewer strives to work with what emerges in the moment, requesting further explication of a laudable brought up by the interviewee. When no obvious laudable is volunteered by the interviewee, the interviewer still manages to turn a particular aspect of interviewee talk into a laudable via "naïve" questioning or uses interviewee talk as a springboard for shifting toward a laudable. Overall, the platform questions create a response slot in which the interviewees are offered, and have been shown to take, the space to promote their agendas on behalf of the institutions they represent.

By detailing a specific question type in news interviews, findings of this study contribute to the growing body of work on question-answer sequences and that on interviewers' questioning practices more specifically. In particular, they make evident the ways in which interviews can be done to forward the interviewees' messaging agendas as they communicate with the public—with a previously undocumented genre of questions in media talk (see also Lo and Yu, this volume).

This supportive role of the interviewer, of course, calls into question the journalistic norms of objectivity and impartiality. Rather than endeavoring to minimize hostility and maintain the fiction of neutrality by speaking on behalf of a third party or packaging questions as "mere questions" through prefaces, presuppositions, and preferences (Heritage & Clayman, 2002), the interviewers in our data play an unapologetically supportive role in helping the interviewees achieve their goal of informing (and educating) the public of the foundation's mission of improving public health. This somewhat unusual journalistic positioning can largely be attributed to the nature of public television, foundations (which the IEs represent) as underwriters of public television programming, and, presumably, the joint aim of advancing the public good that unites the two institutional entities. As such, this study in part answers Clayman's (2013) call to examine the "distinct tasks and practices" associated with "varying genres of news interviews" (p. 656).

Evidently, the relationship between the interviewer and interviewee as representatives of their respective organizations is relevant for, or "procedurally consequential" (Schegloff, 1992, p. 197) in, the practices of questioning. It is also worth noting that in our data this mutually beneficial relationship is made public to the viewer as the interviewer turns to the camera with a "full disclosure" statement either at the beginning or in the midst of an interview. As such, one might argue that at least to some extent the journalist is legitimately becoming a co-messenger with the interviewee. Given this reality, it is perhaps time to broaden our conceptualization of the duties and responsibilities of a TV journalist, and, by extension, the range of professional practices rendered necessary by this broadened conceptualization.

On a practical front, findings of this study provide descriptive and instructive resources for both apprenticing and practicing TV journalists to develop and fine-tune their craft of doing questioning in situations where they are placed in the position of facilitating the informing and marketing agendas of the interviewees. Adding "platform questions" to their toolbox would enhance their technical agility and widen their professional repertoire. In addition, the types of supportive questioning skills detailed in this chapter seem applicable to other contexts that call for some sort of co-messaging, including classroom co-teaching, broadcast talk that involves a host and a guest, such as TV talk shows or radio call-ins (Thornborrow, 2010), and any context in which the task of informing and educating the public is collaboratively accomplished. The practices documented here can hopefully become useful for a wider variety of practitioners beyond public television—as a way of, for example, helping others "get to the point" in any setting that involves communicating with the public. Finally, I hope the fine-grained descriptions of platform questions can help audiences of media talk to recognize moments when journalists are becoming co-messengers, especially where the behind-the-scenes "collusion" between the interviewer and interviewee (as well as the organizational bodies they each represent) is not publicly acknowledged. Such awareness would be beneficial for cultivating critical consumers, and, ultimately, more engaged citizens.

References

Clayman, S. E. (2001). Answers and evasions. *Language in Society, 30,* 403–442.

Clayman, S. E. (2010). Questions in broadcast journalism. In A. F. Freed & S. Ehrlich (Eds.), *"Why do you ask?" The functions of questions in institutional discourse* (pp. 256–278). New York: Oxford University Press.

Clayman, S. E., & Fox, M. P. (2017). Hardballs and softballs: Modulating adversarialness in journalistic questioning. *Journal of Language and Politics, 16*(1), 20–40.

Clayman, S. E., & Heritage, J. (2002). *The news interview: Journalists and public figures on the air.* Cambridge: Cambridge University Press.

Clayman, S. E., & Loeb, L. (2018). Polar questions, response preference, and the tasks of political positioning in journalism. *Research on Language and Social Interaction, 51*(2), 127–144.

Clayman, S. E. (2013). Conversation analysis in the news interview. In J. Sidnell & T. Stivers (Eds.), *The handbook of conversation analysis* (pp. 630–656). Malden, MA: Blackwell Publishing.

Clayman, S. E., & Raymond, C. W. (2015). Modular pivots: A resource for extending turns at talk. *Research on Language and Social Interaction, 48*(4), 388–405.

Ehrlich, S., & Freed, A. (2010). The functions of questions in institutional discourse: An introduction. In A. Freed & S. Ehrlich (Eds.), *Why do you ask? The functions of questions in institutional discourse* (pp. 3–19). New York: Oxford University Press.

Ford, C. (2010). Questioning in meetings: Participation and positioning. In A. Freed & S. Ehrlich (Eds.), *Why do you ask? The functions of questions in institutional discourse* (pp. 211–234). New York: Oxford University Press.

Hepburn, A., & Potter, J. (2010). Interrogating tears. In A. Freed & S. Ehrlich (Eds.), *Why do you ask? The functions of questions in institutional discourse* (pp. 69–86). Oxford: Oxford University Press.

Heritage, J. (2012). The epistemic engine: Sequence organization and territories of knowledge. *Research on Language and Social Interaction, 45*(1), 30–52.

Heritage, J., & Clayman, S. E. (2010). *Talk in action: Interactions, identities, and institutions*. Malden, MA: Wiley-Blackwell.

Heritage, J., & Raymond, G. (2012). Navigating epistemic landscapes: Acquiescence, agency and resistance in responses to polar questions. In J. P. de Ruiter (Ed.), *Questions: Formal, functional and interactional perspectives* (pp. 179–192). Cambridge: Cambridge University Press.

Holmes, J., & Chiles, T. (2010). "Is that right?" Questions and questioning as control devices in the workplace. In A. F. Freed & S. Ehrlich (Eds.), *"Why do you ask?" The function of questions in institutional discourse* (pp. 187–210). Oxford & New York: Oxford University Press.

Jefferson, G. (1983). Notes on some orderliness of overlap onset. *Tilburg Papers in Language and Literature, 28*, 1–28.

Jefferson, G. (1990). List construction as a task and interactional resource. In G. Psathas (Ed.), *Interaction competence* (pp. 63–92). New York: Lawrence Erlbaum.

Koshik, I. (2002). A conversation analytic study of yes/no questions which convey reversed polarity assertions. *Journal of Pragmatics, 34*(12), 1851–1877.

Koshik, I. (2010). Questions that convey information. In A. Freed & S. Ehrlich (Eds.), *Why do you ask? The functions of questions in institutional discourse* (pp. 159–187). Oxford: Oxford University Press.

Labov, W., & Fanshel, D. (1977). *Therapeutic discourse: Psychotherapy as conversation*. Orlando, FL: Academic Press.

Lee, S.-H. (2013). Response design in conversation. In J. Sidnell & T. Stivers (Eds.), *The handbook of conversation analysis* (pp. 415–432). Malden, MA: Blackwell Publishing.

Lerner, G. (1994). Responsive list construction: A conversational resource for accomplishing multifaceted social action. *Journal of Language and Social Psychology, 13*(11), 20–33.

Pomerantz, A. (1980). Telling my side: "Limited access" as a "fishing" device. *Sociological Inquiry, 50*(3–4), 186–198.

Pomerantz, A. (1984). Agreeing and disagreeing with assessments: Some features of preferred/dispreferred turn shapes. In J. Maxwell Atkinson & J. Heritage (Eds.), *Structures of social action: Studies in conversation analysis* (pp. 57–101). New York: Cambridge University Press.

Raymond, G. (2010). Grammar and social relations: Alternative forms of yes/no-type initiating actions in Health Visitor interactions. In A. Freed & S. Ehrlich (Eds.), *Why do you ask? The functions of questions in institutional discourse* (pp. 87–107). Oxford: Oxford University Press.

Sacks, H. (1987). On the preferences for agreement and contiguity in sequences in conversation. In G. Button & J. R. E. Lee (Eds.), *Talk and social organization* (pp. 54–69). Clevedon: Multilingual Matters.

Sacks, H. (1992). *Lectures on conversation: Volumes I and II. Edited by Gail Jefferson, with introductions by Emanuel A. Schegloff*. Cambridge, MA: Blackwell.

Sacks, H., Schegloff, E. A., & Jefferson, G. (1974). A simplest systematics for the organization of turn-taking for conversation. *Language, 50*(4), 696–735.

Schegloff, E. A. (1992). In another context. In A. Duranti & C. Goodwin (Eds.), *Rethinking context: Language as an interactive phenomenon* (pp. 193–227). Cambridge: Cambridge University Press.

Schegloff, E. A. (2007). *Sequence organization in interaction: A primer in conversation analysis* (Vol. 1). Cambridge: Cambridge University Press.

Schegloff, E. A., & Lerner, G. H. (2009). Beginning to respond: Well-prefaced responses to Wh- questions. *Research on Language and Social Interaction, 42*(2), 91–115.

Sidnell, J. (2010). The design and positioning of questions in inquiry testimony. In A. Freed & S. Ehrlich (Eds.), *Why do you ask? The functions of questions in institutional discourse* (pp. 20–41). Oxford: Oxford University Press.

Speer, S. (2010). Pursuing views and testing commitments: Hypothetical questions in the psychiatric assessment of transsexual patents. In A. Freed & S. Ehrlich (Eds.), *Why do you ask? The functions of questions in institutional discourse* (pp. 133–158). Oxford: Oxford University Press.

Stivers, T., & Heritage, J. (2001). Breaking the sequential mould: Answering "more than the question" during comprehensive history taking. *Text, 21*, 151–185.

Stokoe, E., & Edwards, D. (2010). Asking ostensibly silly questions in police-suspect interrogations. In A. Freed & S. Ehrlich (Eds.), *Why do you ask? The functions of questions in institutional discourse* (pp. 108–132). Oxford: Oxford University Press.

Tannen, D. (2007). *Talking voices: Repetition, dialogue, and imagery in conversational discourse.* Cambridge: Cambridge University Press.

Thornborrow, J. (2010). Questions and institutionality in public participation broadcasting. In A. Freed & S. Ehrlich (Eds.), *Why do you ask? The functions of questions in institutional discourse* (pp. 279–296). Oxford: Oxford University Press.

Tracy, K., & Robles, J. (2009). Questions, questioning, and institutional practices: An introduction. *Discourse Studies, 11*(2), 131–152.

3

Enabling Institutional Messaging: TV Journalists' Work with Interviewee Responses

Carol Hoi Yee Lo and Di Yu
Teachers College, Columbia University

Introduction

News interviews, one of the most recognizable and studied forms of public broadcasting, are conducted to inform and educate the audience for the benefit of wider societal interests (Clayman, 2013). Previous conversation analytic (CA) work has noted that the news interview host is positioned as the "tribune of the people" (Clayman, 2002), tasked with the responsibility of maximizing the public's understanding of and knowledge about what may concern them (Clayman & Heritage, 2002a; Hutchby, 1995). Thus far, this work has predominantly focused on interviews with political or public figures (Blum-Kulka, 1983; Clayman & Heritage, 2002b; Ekström, 2001; Fetzer, 2002; Harris, 1991; Hutchby, 1995; Tolson, 2012). Interviews with experts, where a respected expert or authority on a news topic is invited to clarify unfamiliar concepts, provide explanations on technical or semi-technical issues, and shed light on implications of recent developments (Montgomery, 2008), have received much less attention in the literature.

While expert interviews are primarily concerned with disseminating knowledge to the public, it is important to point out that they can also shape public opinion on and citizens' attitudes about social issues (Montgomery, 2008). Given the important social consequences of such interviews, this chapter seeks to understand how institutional messaging—in this case, the advocating of a public health philanthropic foundation's mission and initiatives—is co-constructed by both the interviewer (henceforth IR) and the interviewee (henceforth IE). Our emphasis will be on explicating the IR's journalistic expertise in communicating with the public by enabling institutional messaging.

Past CA literature has shown that the question-answer (Q&A) format is a hallmark of news interview talk; as Heritage and Roth (1995) write, "questioning handles the main interactional and institutional tasks" (p. 1). The turn-taking division of labor is predetermined: The question turn is pre-allocated to the IR whereas the answer turn is pre-allocated to the IE. Since questions in the news interview context can be prefaced by long statements, the IE tends to wait until the IR's question is recognizably complete before offering a response. The IR, on the other hand, cooperates with the IE by withholding the use of receipt or acknowledgment tokens so that an answer consisting of multi-unit turns can be produced. Seen this way, the elaborate questions and answers that are key features of news interviews are in fact collaboratively produced (Clayman, 2013). In addition, comments or assertions from the IR following an IE answer are generally absent in news interviews, though the IR may at times explicitly display understanding on behalf of the audience, thus positioning the audience as the primary recipient of the IE's responses (Clayman, 2013).

In sum, since interviews operate through a pre-allocated turn-taking framework, the IR is restricted to questioning or eliciting information, while the IE is restricted to answering and giving information. Consequently, as Clayman (2013) argues, "turn-taking in the news interview entails a massive reduction in the density of opportunities for action, and in the repertoire of actions that are available to the participants" (p. 636).

In our dataset featuring interviews with health experts, however, we observe that the IR can perform the key action of maximizing the audience's understanding of the topic of discussion by going beyond this Q&A turn-taking structure and operating on the expert's response before initiating a new question. In this chapter, we aim to examine how such IR follow-up turns allow the IR to collaborate with the IE in promoting the foundation and its work as well as educating the public, thus playing a significant role in promoting institutional messaging. Specifically, we show how in expert interviews, despite the presumed epistemic authority of the health expert, the IR can use follow-up turns to (1) provide background or supplemental information and (2) make aspects of foundation messaging concrete.

Data

We draw on four interviews between TV broadcasters and representatives of the Better Living Health Foundation, a philanthropic foundation in the United States. These interviews, featuring two different IRs and four different IEs, were broadcast on local TV stations and are also retrievable online. An important goal of the interviews is to provide the representatives of the foundation with a platform to promote the foundation and its nationwide health mission to the general public. The videos of the four interviews were transcribed in their entirety based on the conventions developed by Jefferson (2004). After an initial line-by-line analysis, we were intrigued by the IR's practices of managing and working with the IE's responses. We decided to conduct a closer examination of the IR's follow-up turns to provide a conversation-analytic description of these practices, which yielded twelve cases that we further categorized into two groups based on the actions performed. In the following section, with the exception of Extract 1, all extracts come from the same interview with the incoming head of the foundation.

Analysis and Findings

In this section, we describe how the IR operates on an IE response to (1) provide background or supplemental information and (2) make aspects of foundation messaging concrete.[1] In terms of sequential position, these two focal practices can be found in what we call a "follow-up" turn. For the purpose of this chapter, we define a follow-up turn as a turn that occurs after an IE response and before the next question is initiated. It is in this specific sequential position where the IR can perform the important action of assisting the IE in facilitating the public's understanding of the foundation's mission and initiatives. It should be noted, however, that some of the follow-up turns in our collection do appear before an IE's response arrives at a possible completion point.

Providing Background or Supplemental Information

The first section of the analysis explores how the IR provides background or supplemental information that is missing from an IE's response in the follow-up turn.

Extract 1 is taken from the beginning of an interview, after the health expert has just been welcomed and introduced as the representative of the Better Living Health Foundation. The IR begins by introducing the working relationship between the IE, the health expert, and the local TV station. He launches the first-pair part of the question-answer sequence in lines 02 and 04–05, where he asks the health expert to first explain to the audience their past collaboration, then discuss a town (i.e., Anytown) in the state where the TV station is based.

(1) Framework for Health

```
01   IR:         we worked together uh over in Anycity {((points
02               at IE))->[ tell ] folks< what that was} and
03   IE:                  [°oh°]
04   IR:         ((finger circling))-we'll bring it over to
05               Anytown. ((points))-[what] was that.=
06   IE:                              [that-]
07               =that was fun that was an opportunity for the
08               foundation to: .h launch and talk about its really
09               ambitious plan to: .h build the Framework for
10               Health in: Anystate and the nation.=an' so it's
11               really an opportunity just to kind of start talking
12               about what that waz: an' bring in some really
13               important .hh thought leaders around tha:t an'
14               it was just a great event.
15   IR:    →    .tch. an' the Framework for Health is uh: uh we
16               should talk about it as being led by Better
17               Living Health Foundation. .h a:nd I would say
18               full disclosure you're underwriting programming,
19               .h on our partners- [for part]ners at Anystate TV
20   IE:                             [°mhm°]
21   IR:         [ and ] for us as well. promoting, and dealing
22   IE:         [°right°.]
23   IR:         with this Framework for Health. what I:S it and
24               why is it important.=
```

The IE's multi-unit turn answer begins with his assessment of their collaboration, *that was fun* in line 07, and is followed by his introduction of the foundation's plan *to build the Framework for Health in Anystate and the nation* (lines 09–10). The IE offers another assessment in line 14, *it was just a great event*, echoing the beginning of his response to the IR's question *what was that*.

The focal lines of this extract begin with line 15, where the IR responds to the answer the IE has just given. Instead of launching a new question, the IR's next turn orients to a specific element mentioned in the answer: *an' the Framework for Health is uh*. The IR first prefaces his follow-up turn with the token *an'*, which allows him to extend and add on to the prior turn, then shines the spotlight on the health mission, a key idea mentioned in the IE's multi-unit answer. The IR then abandons the turn-constructional unit (TCU) and restarts it with *we should talk about it as being led by Better Living Health Foundation*. This follow-up turn clarifies for the audience that the reference *the foundation* in the IE's response (line 08) refers to *Better Living Health Foundation*, especially for viewers who might have missed the formal introduction of the guest. Given that the IR introduces the health expert by first mentioning their past collaboration, the turn also specifies that the health mission is in fact solely led by the foundation. In addition, since the IE has given a long, multi-unit turn response, it can be argued that the IR's follow-up turn aims to direct the audience's attention to the Framework for Health and Better Living Health Foundation—two key topics that both the IR and the IE seek to promote in the interview.

Continuing his turn, the IR goes on to discuss the foundation's and the expert's responsibility and connection to the TV station: *and I would say full disclosure you are underwriting programming for partners on Anystate TV ... promoting and dealing with this Framework for Health* (lines 17–19, 21, and 23). Since the TV station's and the IE's roles and responsibilities are presumably known to both the IR and the IE, this follow-up turn is therefore designed to provide the audience with more supplemental information regarding the foundation and the TV station's working relationship. Observe that the IR describes the information as a *disclosure* to the audience, which could position the TV station and the foundation as transparent to the public, and, therefore, trustworthy. By introducing the IE's responsibility in *promoting and dealing with this Framework for Health*, the IR is also positioning the IE as an authority qualified to answer the next question about the Framework for Health and its importance (lines 23–24).

In sum, the IR's follow-up turn affords him an opportunity to direct the audience's attention to the institution's initiative, Framework for Health, which might have been obscured in the IE's multi-unit turn response. The inserted information about the IE's role in promoting the Framework for Health serves to reinforce the expert's credibility and positions him as a trustworthy source on the initiative. In the following segment, the IR similarly pays close attention to the facts and information in the response and supplies additional background information to reinforce the IE's expert status—even before the response is finished.

At the beginning of Extract 2, the IR asks the IE why he is leaving his current position with the TV station for a new position as the head of the foundation. Instead of offering a reason immediately, the IE begins a multi-unit response by explaining his goals and aspirations to improve health.

(2) the acting head

```
01   IR:         why are you ↑leaving.
02   IE:         .hh you know h- (0.2) I've (0.5) I'm one of
03               these people who- who- who loves a challenge.
04               uh >you know I< focused my whole life on trying
05               to improve health, .h here: and around the globe,
06               >and there're< so many ways that you can
07               engage in tr- and try to do that. .hh I've loved
08               the challenge of- of taking something on in a
09               new way. so:, .h you know, I spent most of my
10               career at the NHC at Anycity >the National<
11               Health Center, looking at public health in a
12               broad way with programs, .h
13   IR:  →     ((arm stretched))-and including, being the acting
14               head of it at one point.
15   IE:         the acting head at the end.
16   IR:         °yup.°
17   IE:         and then:, and then I came here,
```

In lines 09–12, the IE is discussing his career trajectory, which could be heard as paving the way to explain why he is leaving his current position. In lines 09–11, he mentions that he *spent most of* [his] *career at the NHC at Anycity the National Health Center*. Given that the actual account of why he is changing jobs has not been provided, the IE's turn is pragmatically incomplete and therefore has not yet arrived at a possible completion. However, upon the completion of a sentential TCU in line 12, the IR takes a turn in line 13, and, as if speaking on behalf of the IE, adds the position that he held with an *and*-prefaced turn: *and including being the acting head of it at one point.* In his subsequent response, the IE issues an other-correction to clarify that he was *the acting head in the end*, which is met with a quiet, minimal receipt token *yup* from the IR (line 16). Note that the IE's other-correction is not an outright rejection of the additional information about his title, but a modification of the accuracy of the information.

While the IE appears to focus on explicating his responsibilities at the National Health Center in lines 09–12, the IR follow-up turn in lines 13–14 inserts the background information that the IE in fact held a leadership role at the center. Given that the expert is going to be the new head of a foundation focused on promoting health, in highlighting the leadership position that the IE previously held, the IR assists the IE with his self-introduction to the public, helping him avoid self-praise and positioning him as a qualified new leader of the foundation.

In addition to inserting supplementary information that can shine a spotlight on positive attributes and qualifications of the IE, similar to the previous two extracts, the follow-up turn can also supply information that could make the foundation more relatable to the audience. Just prior to Extract 3, the IE has begun to introduce the Better Living Health Foundation, mentioning the foundation's size and mission. As the extract begins, the IR is asking the IE to confirm the foundation's endowment.

(3) owner of Anyteam
```
01   IR:            ((number)) billion dollars is [ what] their endowment
02   IE:                                          [yeah.]
03   IR:            is right?=
04   IE:            =yeah.
05   IR:     →      uh started by:: (0.2) .hh [Joh]nny Smith's
06   IE:                                      [sh- ]
07   IR:     →      grandfather.=[ °syl syl° ]
08   IE:                         =[that's right.] that's right. he
09                  was-
10   IR:     →      the coach of the- the owner of the Anyteam.
```

11	IE:	yea- he was the head of Better Living, an::d
12		he believes strong:ly, .hh that corporations
13		have a responsibility to their community, to
14		their employers, .hh uh to their- to their
15		↑customers.

In line 01, by seeking confirmation of the amount of the foundation's endowment (*((number)) billion dollars is what their endowment is right?*), the IR offers potential evidence to support the IE's previous claim regarding the size of the foundation, thus reinforcing the eminence of the foundation. After the IE confirms the amount (line 04), instead of yielding the floor to the IE so that he can continue describing the foundation, the IR goes on to provide more information regarding the founder of the foundation in line 05. He starts his turn with *uh*, followed by an increment introducing the founder: *started by Johnny Smith's grandfather*. Just as the IE accepts the information and appears ready to provide more information about the founder (Johnny Smith's grandfather) in lines 08–09 (*he was-*), the IR finishes the IE's turn with *the coach of the- the owner of the Anyteam* in line 10. As we can see, the IR appears to be steering the IE's introduction of the foundation; he does so by skillfully inserting information about a famous figure and sports team that are related to the foundation and also associated with the state in which the news program is filmed. While it can be argued that the inserted information that the IR provides might not be necessary for the audience to understand the IE's introduction of the foundation, it does invite the audience to make connections between the foundation and well-known figures who are recognizable in non-health-related contexts. As evidenced by lines 11–15, the IE is prompted by the follow-up turn to introduce the founder of the foundation. The turn therefore contributes to creating opportunities for the IE to talk about the founder and his vision when establishing the foundation.

In all the extracts above, we see that the IR pays close attention to the IE's response and takes advantage of the follow-up turn to add to elements in the IE's response for the benefit of the audience. In terms of turn design, most of the IR's follow-up turns are prefaced by *and*, supplying information related to a specific idea that has been introduced in the prior IE turn. Notably, each follow-up turn allows the IR to either shine the spotlight on a particular item in the IE's previous response—the IE's qualifications, background, or role (Extracts 1 and 2)—or to insert information that might help the audience connect with the foundation (Extract 3). These turns are specifically designed to provide the audience with additional details that may be relevant to already-mentioned topics and to promote further understanding of the information that the IE has provided in his response. Since such interviews with experts aim to promote the foundation and its health initiatives, we argue that the IR's follow-up turns play a key role in facilitating the audience's knowledge about, and, to some extent, trust in both parties—the core of enabling institutional messaging.

Making Aspects of Foundation Messaging Concrete

In addition to providing supplementary information, we find that the IR can also exploit the follow-up turn to make aspects of foundation messaging concrete for the audience. Since the interviewees are representatives of the foundation and experts in the field of public health, it is perhaps unsurprising that when introducing the foundation's mission and health initiative, their responses can feature catchphrases and jargon common in the domain of public health (e.g., funding, research, access). In his analysis of news interviews, Heritage (1985) has noted that the IR's formulations of the IE's response can be "inferentially elaborative" as they can explicitly highlight elements from the response as important details to be focused on (p. 103). In the case of interviews with experts, we argue that the IR can employ such formulations in the follow-up turn to make foundation messaging come to life for the audience, in particular formulations of the problems that the foundation seeks to address and the solutions that it proposes.

In Extract 4, we see the IR and the IE discussing the details of the foundation's programs and funded projects to improve public health. Right before this segment, the IR is pursuing a response from the IE regarding how he, as the head of the foundation, can effect substantial changes in public health. In response, the IE begins with an acknowledgment that *he has a lot to learn*.

(4) food money

```
01   IR:       >you're talking about [huge social economic
02   IE:                              [I have a
03   IR:       change.<]
04   IE:             lot  ] to learn. I start next week, and I've
05                 a lot to learn about what's going on.=but some
06                 is done through- .h through the programs that
07                 we fund. so there's a lot of focus on childhood
08                 obesity for example. the foundation pledged
09                 ((number)) billion dollars over a ten year period.
10                 that's real money.
11   IR:    →   so does that mean giving people food money?
12   IE:       [no what that- ]
13   IR:    →   [to eat healthy?]
14   IE:       what that's doing is- a lot of that money is- is
15                 working in the schools, and teaching children,
16                 .hh you know putting- putting programs around
17                 physical activity physical fitness. .h putting
18                 programs in to make sure school lunches are
19                 healthy. .hh getting at that component of- of-
20                 of the- you know live learn work play [uh- uh-]
21   IR:                                                 [°mhm.°]
```

After prefacing his response to the IR's question about how to effect change in public health with *I have a lot to learn. I start next week* (lines 02 and 04), the IE provides an example of how the foundation has devoted money to combat childhood obesity in lines 05–10. Notice that the IE characterizes the foundation's solution as a proposed allocation of funds over time: *the foundation pledged ((number)) billion dollars over a ten year period*. Positioned right after the IE's answer, the IR's understanding-check in line 11, which begins with a summative *so*, transforms a pledge of significant funding into the concrete action of *giving people food money* followed by an increment *to eat healthy* (line 13). We argue that this candidate understanding in the follow-up turn performs two important actions: First, it translates *((number)) billion dollars* and *real money* into a candidate realization of such an initiative, *food money*. Second, it invites the IE to reject or accept the suggested initiative (line 14), thereby creating an opportunity for his further elaboration on what the foundation can really do to help with the childhood obesity epidemic. As evidenced in lines 14–20, the IE indeed provides a list of actions detailing how the money will be spent as an indirect way to reject the IR's proposal of *giving people food money*. This follow-up turn, then, facilitates the promotion of the institution's messages by proposing a concrete realization of the foundation's mission, which can then be accepted, rejected, or modified by the IE.

While in the previous extract, the IR's follow-up turn helps specify a foundation proposed solution, in the next two extracts, the IR's follow-up turns work to underscore the reality of the problems the foundation seeks to address for the audience. As Extract 5 begins, the IR suggests delving into the foundation's mission. In lines 01–03, he asks the IE to explain how the foundation seeks to improve the health of Americans and how the enormous amount of funding will be spent. The focal point is in line 27, where the IR completes the IE's multi-unit turn.

(5) that exists

```
01   IR:      let's get in the weeds of that a little bit. what
02            does that mean try to improve the health of-
03            of Americans. [AN:D] how do you do that with
04   IE:                    [ yeah.]
05   IR:      >((number)) million dollars a year< because,
06            when you talk about healthcare in general we're
07            talking about billions of dollars. [°(      )°   ]
08   IE:                                        [ yeah. well, I- ]
09            think, >you know,< when you look at what the
10            Better Living Health Foundation is trying to
11            do, they- they talk about building a Framework
12            for Health. and what that- that idea is is- that health
13            isn't just something that takes place between
14            you and your- your doctor. .hh health- health
15            occur:s through what takes place where you work,
16            where you live, where your children learn, and
17            where they play. .h and so it's about trying to
18            ensure that all of those things are contributing
19            to the health of people here. .hh do people-
20            >you know I-< I've been working for seven
21            years in a clinic up in ↑Anycity. .hh an::d I
```

```
22                    talked to my patients about well exercise y-
23                    all the stuff I do on the air here. well what if
24                    there's no access to fresh fruits and vegetables.
25                    or the streets aren't safe for your kid to go
26                    outside [and play.]
27   IR:   →               [and that ]exists.
28   IE:          [that EXISTS.]        [ exactly.    ]
29   IR:   →      [  in  this ci ]ty and [in a lot of big] cities.
30   IE:          and, those things are critically important to
31                    ↑health and so as a foundation, what we're
32                    ((continues))
```

In response to the IR's question, the IE starts by introducing and defining the Framework for Health (lines 08–12). To explain what the Framework for Health entails, the IE begins to discuss his personal experience working in a clinic in line 20, particularly how he advised his patients: *I talked to my patients about well exercise y- all the stuff I do on the air here* (lines 21–23). He then contrasts his advice with the potential problem of access and safety, framed as a hypothetical: *well what if there's no access to fresh fruits and vegetables or the streets aren't safe for your kid to go outside and play* (lines 23–26). Also note that the use of *your kid* indicates a shift in footing; the IE is directing the rhetorical question regarding access and safety to the audience.

As the sentential TCU that begins in line 25 arrives at a possible completion point in line 26 (*or the streets aren't safe for your kid to go outside*), the IR takes the next turn in line 27, overlapping with the IE who produces further talk past the possible completion point at line 28. Here, the IR extends the IE's turn by supplying an *and*-prefaced clause and completes the IE's turn (*and that exists*). This pre-emptive completion (Lerner, 2004) of his turn is immediately taken up by the IE, who repeats *that exists* in high volume to display strong agreement in line 28. Through the collaborative completion, the IR transforms what could be heard as a rhetorical question (*well what if*) into an assertion, highlighting the reality of the problem (*that exists*). While the ideas of fresh food and street safety mentioned in the IE's response in lines 23–26 are everyday concepts, the IR's work of reframing the ideas of lacking access to fresh food and unsafe streets prompts the audience to view them as real, imminent issues rather than hypothetical, "what if" problems.

Also note that while the IE has been discussing issues in Anycity (lines 20–22), the IR's continuation of his collaborative completion in line 29, in which he appends a prepositional phrase, *in this city and a lot of big cities*, broadens the geographic scope of discussion. As a result, the audience in other cities and perhaps parts of the country can also relate to the problem being discussed. Since the IE is explaining the foundation's initiative, Framework for Health, it can also be argued that the IR is assisting the IE with helping the audience relate to the problem, appreciate the scope of the problem, and understand what the foundation's initiative entails.

A similar pattern of the IR concretizing a potential, hypothetical issue mentioned in the IE's response can be observed in Extract 6 as well. On the same topic of how the foundation funds programs, the IE is now responding to the IR's question regarding whether the foundation is giving people food money (see also Extract 4).

(6) groceries at the bodega

```
01   IR:          so does that mean giving people food money?
02   IE:          [no what that- ]
03   IR:          [to eat healthy?]
04   IE:          what that's doing is a lot of that money is- is
05                working in the schools, and teaching children,
06                .hh you know putting- putting programs around
07                physical activity physical fitness. .h putting
08                programs in to make sure school lunches are
09                healthy. .hh getting at that component of- of-
10                of the- you know live learn work play [uh- uh-]
11   IR:                                                [°mhm.°]
12   IE:          uh piece of it. .hh it's funding research to see
13                what can you do to: to: stimulate the: the: the
14                access to those things.=how do ya get fresh
15                fruits and vegetables into the corner .h corner
16                ↑store, you know [   in the bodega.   ]
17   IR:    →                      [cos a lot of people] buy
18                their groceries at the bodega [ which does not- ]
19   IE:                                        [   e x a c t l y ]
20   IR:    →     not necessarily have, [the kind of healthy] food.
21   IE:                                [    yeah so- so    ]
```

22	how do you make sure that- that fresh fruits
23	and vegetables are what they see when they
24	walk in, .h rather than walking in and seeing
25	things that aren't so healthy.

In line 04, the IE begins his response by offering a list of how the foundation is going to spend money, focusing mostly on schools and children (lines 04–10). In line 12, the IE goes on to describe the type of research that the foundation funds. In lines 14–16, the IE offers an example of a potential research question: *how do ya get fresh fruits and vegetables into the corner corner store*, a complete sentential TCU; a possible completion point has thus arrived. Similar to Extract 5, the IE's use of the pronoun *you* (lines 13 and 14) subtly shifts the footing of his answer mid-turn to addressing the audience. After the token *you know* in line 16, the IR takes the next turn in line 17, providing a dependent clause beginning with the subordinator *cos* (because), an increment to the IE's turn supplying the reason that the IE has implied but has not yet provided explicitly: *cos a lot of people buy their groceries at the bodega which does not- not necessarily have the kind of healthy food* (lines 17–18 and 20). Considering that the IE has been discussing what courses of action will be taken but not why they need to be pursued, the account provided by the IR, to a large extent, reformulates the IE's suggested research question into a more concrete, existing problem (*a lot of people buy their groceries at the bodega*). This shift in perspective can encourage the audience to confront the reality of the problem, and, consequently, appreciate the importance of the foundation's initiative.

In sum, in the follow-up turns we have examined in Extracts 5 and 6, we see that the IR co-authors with the IE by confirming the reality and expanding the scope of a problem that the IE has brought up in his response (Extract 5) or supplying concrete reasons behind the foundation's concerns (Extract 6). While Lerner (2004) points out that such collaborative completions have the potential to advance or alter the action of the original speaker's turn, we notice that the IR's completions are immediately and enthusiastically accepted by the IE, showing that such completions are designedly aligning and affiliative in contributing to promoting the foundation's mission.

Discussion and Conclusion

In this chapter, we have examined how the IR can exploit what we call a "follow-up" turn—the sequential space between the receipt of an answer and the launch of the next question—in order to enable institutional messaging. Specifically, we have shown that the IR can collaborate with the IE to promote an institution's mission and initiatives through two practices, namely, providing background or supplemental information and making aspects of foundation messaging concrete. With regard to the first practice, as we have demonstrated in Extracts 1–3, after the IE's response, the IR can use a follow-up turn to provide background or supplemental information, often prefacing the turn with the token *and* and appending the information to a specific part of the IE's response. This additional information, which is often related to an element in the IE's long, multi-unit response, draws the audience's attention to that specific element and supplies relevant information that might be missing. This practice illustrates how the IR strives for factual accuracy (Extracts 1–2) and enabling the audience to "connect the dots" (Extract 3), which in turn maximizes the audience's knowledge of the foundation.

In the case of the second practice, the IR produces brief follow-up turns to underscore certain elements of the IE's response in order to make them explicit or concrete. These turns can take the form of a candidate understanding that transforms the solution of providing a large sum of funding into a concrete use of that funding (Extract 4). They can also be collaborative completions that reframe hypothetical issues or research proposals mentioned in the IE's talk into real problems that the audience confronts (Extracts 5–6). While it should be pointed out that the IE's talk does not always include specialized terms per se, the IR does endeavor to explicate and animate IE messaging for the audience. In this way, the IR's follow-up turns play a key role in facilitating the audience's understanding of initiatives pertaining to public health. We argue that the core of enabling institutional messaging, as the IRs in our dataset have demonstrated, is to enable the foundation's mission and initiatives to resonate with the audience, and this can be effectively done by offering concrete realizations of common catchphrases or jargon such as "fund research" and "stimulate access."

In sum, our chapter addresses Clayman's (2013) call for research on distinct tasks and practices in specific genres of news interviews by examining interviewers' journalistic expertise in working with responses in interviews with health experts, who are also representatives of a philanthropic foundation. Our analysis contributes to a more nuanced understanding of how the participants orient to designing talk for the viewing public and how the finesse in the IR's follow-up turn design plays a role in informing and educating the audience regarding public health. While past work on news interviews with politicians has underscored the IR's role in holding the public figure accountable through questioning (Clayman, 2002), we hope to have illustrated that in the context of interviewing an expert, holding the public figure accountable is not a driving concern. Rather, it is informing and educating the public that becomes the first-order action. In our data, the IR often takes the next turn as soon as an abstract idea is mentioned, at times even before the IE's turn arrives at a transition-relevance place. This suggests that offering an interpretation might take priority over allowing the IE to finish a multi-unit turn. In fact, the IR's use of follow-up turns is reminiscent of how a teacher might work with a student's response in a classroom. Given that both the teacher and the IR seek to elucidate difficult concepts and make ideas come alive, the "follow-up" turn performs functions similar to the teacher's feedback turn (Lee, 2007; Mehan, 1979; Sinclair & Coulthard, 1975). Relatedly, Drew (1992), in his analysis of courtroom interaction, discusses "the power of summary," as the attorney can "pull together evidence and draw conclusions" (p. 507)—a sequential advantage resulting from the pre-allocated question-answer format of the courtroom. We hope to have shown that the same advantage can also be observed in the data in our study, where the IR can exploit "the power of summary" for the benefit of the general audience.

On a more practical front, our findings have important implications for journalism training. It is important to underscore that journalistic professionalism can be enacted in ways beyond going adversarial or maintaining neutrality (Clayman & Heritage, 2002b) (see also Waring, this volume). Our study has demonstrated the great communicative finesse that journalists display, in terms of both turn-taking and question design, when collaborating with the interviewee to communicate important ideas to the public. For the interviewees, who represent the institution, our findings invite the recognition that the IR can in fact be their collaborator in delivering institutional messaging. This study, then, enables journalists-in-training to see how their practices should vary at a fine-grained level according to the overarching goal of the interview, and how conveying institutional messages to the public can be skillfully done.

Note

1   Preliminary analysis of Extracts 1, 3, and 4 appeared in Lo and Yu (2018).

References

Blum-Kulka, S. (1983). The dynamics of political interviews. *Text, 3*(2), 131–153.

Clayman, S. E. (2002). Tribune of the people: Maintaining the legitimacy of aggressive journalism. *Media, Culture & Society, 24*(2), 197–216.

Clayman, S. E. (2013). Conversation analysis in the news interview. In J. Sidnell & T. Stivers (Eds.), *The handbook of conversation analysis* (pp. 630–656). Malden, MA: Blackwell Publishing.

Clayman, S. E., & Heritage, J. (2002a). *The news interview: Journalists and public figures on the air*. Cambridge: Cambridge University Press.

Clayman, S. E., & Heritage (2002b). Questioning presidents: Journalistic deference and adversarialness in the press conferences of U.S. Presidents Eisenhower and Reagan. *Journal of Communication, 52*(4), 749–775.

Drew, P. (1992). Contested evidence in courtroom cross-examination: The case of a trial for rape. In P. Drew & J. Heritage (Eds.), *Talk at work: Interaction in institutional settings* (pp. 470–520). Cambridge: Cambridge University Press.

Ekström, M. (2001). Politicians interviewed on television news. *Discourse and Society, 12*, 563–584.

Fetzer, A. (2002). 'Put bluntly, you have something of a credibility problem': Sincerity and credibility in political interviews. In P. Chilton & C. Schäffner (Eds.), *Politics as talk and text: Analytic approaches to political discourse* (pp. 173–201). Amsterdam: John Benjamins.

Harris, S. (1991). Evasive action: How politicians respond to questions in political interviews. In P. Scannell (Ed.), *Broadcast talk* (pp. 76–99). London: Sage.

Heritage, J. (1985). Analyzing news interviews: Aspects of the production of talk for an overhearing audience. In T. A. Van Dijk (Ed.), *Handbook of discourse analysis* (Vol. 3) (pp. 95–119). New York: Academic Press.

Heritage, J., & Roth, A. (1995). Grammar and institution: Questions and questioning in the broadcast news interview. *Research on Language and Social Interaction, 28*, 1–60.

Hutchby, I. (1995). Aspects of recipient design in expert advice giving on call in radio. *Discourse Processes, 19*(2), 219–238.

Jefferson, G. (2004). Glossary of transcript symbols with an introduction. In G. Lerner (Ed.), *Conversation analysis: Studies from the first generation* (pp. 13–31). Amsterdam: John Benjamins.

Lee, Y.-A. (2007). Third turn position in teacher talk: Contingency and the work of teaching. *Journal of Pragmatics, 39*, 1204–1230.

Lerner, G. H. (2004). Collaborative turn sequences. In G. H. Lerner (Ed.), *Conversation analysis: Studies from the first generation* (pp. 225–256). Amsterdam: John Benjamins.

Lo, C., & Yu, D. (2018). Enabling institutional messaging: TV journalists' work with interviewee responses. *Studies in Applied Linguistics & TESOL, 18*(1), 36–43.

Mehan, H. (1979). *Learning lessons: Social organization in the classroom*. Cambridge, MA: Harvard University Press.

Montgomery, M. (2008). The discourse of broadcast news interview. *Journalism Studies, 9*(2), 260–277.

Sinclair, J. M., & Coulthard, M. (1975). *Towards an analysis of discourse: The English used by teachers and pupils*. London: Oxford University Press.

Tolson, A. (2012). "You'll need a miracle to win this election" (J. Paxman 2005): Interviewer assertiveness in UK general elections 1983–2010. *Discourse, Context & Media, 1*(1), 45–53.

4

Constructing the Audience in Media Interviews

Nadja Tadic and Di Yu
Teachers College, Columbia University

Introduction

Media interviews have long been a focus of discourse analytic research, with studies exploring interviews in terms of their structure, questioning and answering practices, and issues of expertise and ideology (e.g., Armon, 2016; Clayman & Heritage, 2002; Tilney, 2015). However, the role of the audience, while recognized as integral (Clayman, 2015), is still fairly under-explored. Prior conversation analytic research has examined how interviewers frame the interview as being conducted for the benefit of an audience (Clayman, 2013) by regularly positioning the audience as ratified overhearers (Goffman, 1981). Interviewers, for instance, orient to the audience through explicit references to it (Clayman, 2002, 2010), full-form references to the interviewees (Clayman, 1989), avoidance of receipt tokens during interviewees' extended turns, and explicit displays of understanding of interviewees' responses, thus helping clarify these responses for the audience (Clayman, 2010; Heritage, 1985).

While this research on interviewers' practices for constructing an audience has been extremely fruitful, who exactly *interviewees* position as their intended audience remains unexamined. To address this gap, in this chapter we explore how representatives of one philanthropic foundation construct their audience as specific members of the public during media interviews. Through linguistic choices that display their expectations of who their audience members are, what knowledge and experiences they possess, and what their goals and values might be, the interviewees appear to inform and engage a particular subset of the general population in their promotional agenda.

Data

Our data consist of video recordings of six publicly available media interviews conducted with representatives of a philanthropic foundation in the United States. Four different interviewers and eight different interviewees participated in these six interviews; three of the interviews were conducted by the same interviewer, and two of the interviews were conducted with two interviewees at the same time. The six excerpts in this chapter come from five different interviews conducted by three different interviewers. The interviews, typically around ten minutes in length or shorter, were broadcast on local television stations and were both informational and promotional in nature, giving the foundation an outlet to present and involve the public in their most recent ventures in improving public health. Within this collection of interviews, we identified thirty-five instances in which the interviewees appeared to orient to the audience through person references, place references, and activity formulations. Below, we examine how these references and formulations are designed and what they suggest about who is included in and excluded from the foundation's messaging on public health. As our initial line-by-line analysis suggested patterns in terms of which social groups were included in and excluded from the foundation's messaging, we also adopted a critical perspective for a more nuanced exploration of the ideologies underlying this messaging.

Analysis and Findings

In our examination of how interviewees orient to viewers through person references, place references, and activity formulations, we identified the constructed audience as: actively engaged middle-class members of the local (or national) community. We borrow the term "community" from the representatives themselves, who regularly encourage their viewers to *build a sense of community*. This category seems to entail a group of people connected to each other and to the foundation through: (1) shared spaces; (2) shared experiences, values, and concerns; and (3) a shared ability to address those concerns. We would like to note that, while these features might not define a community in other circumstances, they do appear to constitute the participants' underlying "definition" of community in the data.

In the following subsections, we explore how each of these characteristics is enacted in the interviewees' linguistic choices. In each subsection, we examine an instance in which certain members of the general public are included in the foundation's messaging and an instance in which other members are excluded from it. Collectively, these subtle means of inclusion and exclusion help define who the foundation's intended audience is and how this audience might be shaping the foundation representatives' interview contributions.

Audience as Members of a Community

In their interviews, foundation representatives typically position their audience as members of a national or local community. As the foundation's focus is on health within the United States and as the interviews under examination were conducted on local U.S. television stations, the audience is unsurprisingly constructed as local and/or national. However, beyond orienting to the geographical location of the audience, the foundation representatives also enact a close connection with their viewers, thus involving the audience in their current projects and creating a sense of community in their messaging.

We can see the construction of the audience as a community in the first extract, where the interviewee (IE) is answering a question about the foundation's approach to childhood obesity. In delivering her answer, the interviewee frames the issue of childhood obesity as a national one, which all members of the country should address together.

(1) in this country
```
    01   IR:        it says that a Framework for Health means
    02              reversing (.) childhood obesity
    03              epidemic.=break that down.=what d'es that
    04              mean.
```

05	IE:	→	.hhh fo:r more than thirty years the:
06		→	trajectory of obesity in this country for kids
07			has been going {like that.-((*rt hand showing*
08			*upward trajectory*))} .hh <u>w</u>e know that when
09			kids enter adulthood overweight or obese,
10			they have a <u>m</u>uch higher probability of
11			having chronic illnesses like <u>h</u>eart disease,
12			diabetes. and <u>th</u>at leads to: disabilities and
13			early deaths.=so that (.) by having <u>so</u> many
14			kids u:h with uh- overweight or obesity as
15		→	part of their (.) makeup? <u>w</u>e may be the first
16		→	country that uh uh- first generation that lives
17			d- sicker and dies younger than (.) their
18			parents. and <u>th</u>at is something that has never
19			been part of the way we <u>th</u>ought about
20		→	health in this country.

As he introduces the topic of childhood obesity (lines 01–04), the interviewer (IR) treats it as a generic issue which the audience is not expected to be familiar with (note the absence of the definite article *the* in the phrase *childhood obesity epidemic*, lines 02–03). However, the interviewee in her answer reframes the issue as not only implicitly familiar to but highly relevant for the U.S. audience as a community. First of all, she describes the issue not as new but as one that has existed for a considerable period of time (line 05, *more than thirty years*) and would, therefore, be familiar to the viewers. She further locates the issue as existing not generally "out there" but specifically in the United States (line 06, *obesity in this country*). Here, her use of the proximal deictic form *this* (lines 06 and 20) more closely ties the issue to the United States and its citizens, and by extension to the program's U.S.-based audience. Finally, the interviewee frames the issue of childhood obesity as even more directly relevant to the audience through her use of the first-person plural pronoun *we* (lines 15 and 19), thus positioning herself, the foundation, and the audience as a united group concerned with childhood obesity. The interviewee thus manages to shift what was originally introduced as a generic, unfamiliar issue into a concern highly relevant for both the foundation and a specific community—the U.S. audience.

Foundation representatives might also narrow down their audience further by addressing smaller communities within the United States (e.g., populations of specific states, counties, and cities). However, just as they construct their viewers as a unified community, representatives at times also implicitly exclude certain populations from that community. An example of such implicit exclusion can be seen in the next extract, where the interviewee is focusing on the foundation's Framework for Health initiative in a specific city in the United States—Anytown—which has a population that is approximately 90 percent Hispanic and Black and a median household income of around $25,000 (Data USA, n.d.). In introducing the foundation's Framework for Health initiative in Anytown, the interviewee describes his personal connection to this city; however, he indirectly excludes the city's population from the current interview audience.

(2) you have parents there and people there

```
01    IR:            [so what's your] connection to [Anytown.]
02    IE:                                           [Anytown ]
03                   so I- I came to Anytown- I grew up in Othertown
04                   which is only a couple of miles from
05                   Anytown geographically but (.) big jump ge-
06       →           socioeconomically an' I came to Anytown .hh
07                   fresh out of nursing school, I: became a school
08                   nurse there, .hh I was about twenty six years
09       →           o:ld, and it's this place where I ended up
10                   buying a house,
11    IR:            right.
12    IE:            I met my wife, I had my first child, I work
13                   there I started a youth development group there,
14       →           and I uh felt a very close connection to this
15                   place which is .hh in many ways it's- it's a
16                   place that's like- (en)like Othertown, >I mean<
17       →           you have parents there and people there that
18                   .h uh:: wanna raise their families and have
19                   kids there really wanna ha:ve interesting an'
20                   .h uh::m constructive adulthoods, um but there's
21                   these barriers that kinda get in the way an' in
22                   Anytown, .hh really brings you kind of
23                   [ face to face with what] these barriers are.
24    IR:            [ what kind of barriers.]
```

The interviewee builds a connection to Anytown and its population by describing his own personal experiences. He enacts an emotional closeness to the city by recounting some of the major life moments he experienced there (lines 10, 12–13) and a physical closeness to it by using the verb *came* (line 06) and the proximal deictic *this place* (lines 09 and 14–15). However, despite this expressed emotional and physical connection to Anytown, the interviewee also implicitly creates a distance from the city and its population. First, he positions himself as originally a non-member of Anytown: He notes that he grew up in the neighboring Othertown, which is *a big jump socioeconomically* from Anytown (lines 05–06), being over 65 percent White and having a median household income of approximately $85,000 (Data USA, n.d.). Second, the interviewee repeatedly refers to Anytown and its population with the distal deictic *there* (lines 08, 13, 17, 19), suggesting a physical distance between Anytown and the current interview context. Finally, he positions members of Anytown as objects or figures (Goffman, 1981) of his messaging rather than addressed hearers. Specifically, in line 17 (*you have parents there and people there*), the interviewee frames the population of Anytown as a feature of this city which needs to be introduced and explained to his addressed audience (*you*). Therefore, unlike in the previous extract, where the interviewee positioned the population impacted by her messaging as her audience (line 15, *this country*, line 20, *we*), here the interviewee orients to the Anytown population as figures distant, separate, and unfamiliar to his intended audience.

It is interesting that *parents there and people there* (line 17), who are excluded from the audience, are still positioned as sharing the interviewee's social values. They have aspirations to *raise their families* and *have interesting and constructive adulthoods* (lines 18–20)—aspirations that the interviewee himself managed to realize (lines 10, 12–13). However, it appears that people who do not (yet) enact those social values in their daily lives do not belong to an audience concerned with the foundation's messaging on the Framework for Health in Anytown, nor do they have any active role in working against the *barriers* that are keeping them from fully realizing these values. The foundation, therefore, appears to be constructing their audience as a *middle-class* national or local community, implicitly excluding as recipients of their messaging groups who are not (yet) part of the middle class. How foundation representatives draw on social values to construct their audience as belonging to the middle class is examined more closely in the next section.

Audience as Espousing Middle-class Values

As representatives promote the foundation's health projects, they identify specific goals of these projects, such as providing members of the local community with access to safe physical exercise spaces and healthy food choices. These goals are articulated quite consistently through reference to particular social categories and attributes, ones which, far from being "neutral," underscore particular social values: middle-class values, to be exact. And this implicit integration of middle-class values in the foundation's messaging helps us further specify the intended audience as members of the middle-class local community.

Extract 3 illustrates how one foundation representative (IE) draws on middle-class values to outline the foundation's goals and position a specific population as her audience. The interviewee is answering a question about what makes certain state counties healthy (lines 01–05). As she delivers her response, she gradually transitions from addressing a general to a more specific audience.

(3) a good job

```
01   IR:        .tch and- and what is it about these counties
02              here that set them apart when it comes to .h
03              uh evaluating health standards.=is it the
04              access, is it the environment, take- take us
05              through what you think makes it so healthy.
06              (0.5)
07   IE:        .h sure it- you know a lot of times that's
08              what people think. they think access to
09              quality care is the most important thing
10              about what drives our health. and certainly
11              .hh it i:s important but even more important
12              are those factors that I was talking about
13  →           earlier. like uhm can kids get a good high
14  →           school education, can people get a good job,
15  →           do people feel safe in their neighborhood.
16  →           .hh uhm do people have the opportunity to
17  →           wa:lk and bi:ke and be physically active. .hh
18              and so it's this vari:ety of factors all coming
19  →           together that really create health in your
20              community.
```

At the start of her response, the interviewee refers to common misconceptions that *people*, in a very general sense, have about health (line 08). However, as she goes on to introduce the foundation's approach to health, she narrows down those concerned by formulating health in terms of specific social categories and attributes: children's education, quality employment, neighborhood safety, and outdoor physical activity (lines 13–17). These formulations hold presuppositions about the experiences, concerns, and values of the audience for whom the interviewee's explanation is designed: These are career-oriented people with children, who (want to) live and engage in recreational physical activity in safe neighborhoods. The viewers are further constructed as belonging to a unified community addressed directly by the interviewee (lines 19–20, *your community*). In other words, a community of professionals who value quality education for their children, neighborhood safety, and physical recreation become the audience.

Such implicit construction of the audience also suggests who might be excluded from it—for example, people who do not have children and/or are not primarily concerned with quality employment, neighborhood safety, or physical recreation. Particular members of the general population are occasionally excluded more directly from the foundation's messaging, as we can see in the next extract, where the interviewee is addressing the foundation's project investments.

(4) that exists

```
01   IR:         >((number)) dollars a year< because,
02               when you talk about healthcare in general
03               we're talking about billions of dollars.
04               [°(      )°   ]
05   IE:         [ yeah. well, I- ] think, >you know<, when
06               you look at what the Better Living Health
07               Foundation is trying to do, they- they talk
08               about building a Framework for Health. and
09               what that- that idea is is- that health isn't just
10   →           something that takes place between you and
11               your- your doctor. .hh health- health occur:s
12   →           through what takes place where you work,
13   →           where you live, where your children learn,
```

14			and where they play. .h and so it's about
15			trying to ensure that <u>all</u> of those things are
16			contributing to the health of people here. .hh
17			do people- >you know I-< I've been
18			working for seven years in a clinic up in-
19			Anycity. .hh an::d I talked to my patients
20			about well exercise y- all the stuff I do on
21		→	the air here. well what if there's no access to
22		→	fresh fruits and vegetables. or the streets
23		→	aren't safe for your kid to go outside
24			[and play.]
25	IR:	→	[and that] exists.
26	IE:		[that EXISTS.]
27	IR:		[in this ci]ty and [a lot of big] cities.
28	IE:		[exactly.]
29			and, th<u>o</u>se things are critically important to
30			health and so as a foun<u>d</u>ation, what we're
31			((*continues*))

After outlining the overall purpose of the foundation's current project in lines 05–14, the interviewee summarizes the foundation's goals as concerned with improving the health of *people here*, establishing the relevance of his message for the U.S.-based (or potentially more local) audience with the generic noun *people* and the proximal deictic *here*. The interviewee then further frames the foundation's work as relevant for specific members of the community—those concerned with having *access to fresh fruits and vegetables* and parents (lines 21–23). Interestingly, while the interviewee positions any listener as concerned with these issues (*there's*, line 21; *your kid*, line 23), these experiences are phrased as entirely hypothetical (*what if*, line 21). What's more, beyond being hypothetical, they are treated as necessitating quite an imaginative leap from the audience: Both the interviewer and the interviewee explicitly reassure the audience that lack of access to nutrition and safety is a reality for some people (*that exists,* lines 25 and 26). In this way, they orient to the audience as unfamiliar with areas in which safety and healthy food options are not a given. We consequently see the generic local audience gradually becoming more specific, including people concerned with and accustomed to good nutrition and safety, and excluding those who lack access to these lifestyle conditions. The foundation, thus, implicitly reinforces middle-class values in their messaging and implicitly constructs their audience as members of the middle-class local community. And the groups most afflicted by the public-health issues discussed in the foundation's messaging are inadvertently excluded from its addressed recipients.

Audience as Agents of Change

Finally, foundation representatives design their talk for an audience that can take an active role in the projects they are promoting. As the purpose of these interviews is generally to both inform and engage the public in the foundation's ventures, it is not surprising that representatives position the audience as capable of actively participating. However, when we examine who is positioned in this way, we once again notice that it is not the general population but a specific subset of the population that the foundation constructs as their intended audience. More specifically, foundation representatives typically position professionals, educators, and parents as agents of health in local communities. We can see how these social categories are given agency as they are invited to participate in the foundation's Framework for Health project in Extract 5 (taken from the same interview as Extract 1). In the extract, the interviewee (IE) is answering a question about the foundation's role in helping local groups promote health in their communities (01–05), and, as she does so, she introduces the notion of community *leaders* playing a key role.

(5) urban planner

01	IR:		is t̲hat the role of the foundation to partner
02			with .hh groups who're in the community
03			doing these things. an' help them do what
04			they m̲ay not be able t' do for themselves
05			>cuz they don't have< the resources?
06	IE:		that's- that's c̲ertainly a big part of it? .hh
07		→	another big part of it is getting leaders who
08			do̲n't think of themselves as being a part of
09			creating a healthy environment. .hh to see:
10			their wo̲rk as helping people be healthier.
11		→	if you a:re u:m in- an urban planner. o:r an

```
12   →    architect. you may not think of yourself as
13   →    someone who promotes health. .hh but, step
14   →    back for a moment. and consider whether
15        or not there're sidewalks, or there're
16        buildings that encourage physical activity?
17        that's a:ll in the domain of architects and
18        urban planners. .hh so part of what we do
19        at the foundation is .hhh as you say find
20        people who are already doing the good
21        [works.]
22  IR:   [mm:, ]
```

When she initially introduces *leaders*, the interviewee uses a somewhat vague post-modifier to narrow down the reference: *leaders who don't think of themselves as being a part of creating a healthy environment* (lines 07–09). At this point, a rather wide subset of the population could potentially identify with being leaders in the interviewee's sense of the word. However, the interviewee then offers example categories that reveal certain implicit attributes of bona fide leaders. She formulates leaders as *urban planners* or *architects*—two professional categories that typically require advanced education degrees and entail officially approved, large-scale civic design and construction. As they are introduced, these "model" leaders are addressed directly by the interviewee and guided in terms of how they could promote health in their local communities (lines 11–18, *if you are um in- urban planner. or an architect ... consider whether or not there're sidewalks ...*). In this way, the interviewee actively involves a specific type of viewer in the foundation's work—a highly educated professional capable of shaping the physical space of communities on a larger scale.

As mentioned, foundation representatives position other members of the population, such as parents and educators, as potential contributors to community health as well. An example of parents having an active role in the foundation's health agenda can be seen in our final example, which also illustrates a subset of the population that apparently cannot play an active role in the foundation's mission and is thus implicitly excluded from the audience of the foundation's messaging. In this extract, the interviewee is answering a question about a data analysis tool, called County Health Project, which the foundation is promoting. In explaining the purpose of this tool, the interviewee notes its potential use in understanding the state of education, employment, and child poverty across counties (lines 04–05). As she does so, she first uses a generic *you* to address an audience of potential users of this tool (line 02), before further narrowing down the intended, agentive audience.

(6) kids living in poverty

```
01   IE:           .hh so they can- actually County Health
02         →       Project will tell you all of the different
03                 things that we've been talking about.
04                 education, unemployment. .hh children- the
05                 percentage of children living in poverty.
06         →       we have: la:rge numbers of kids living in
07                 poverty in the state, .hh an' we know that
08                 that sets them up as uh:: that the odds are
09                 against them from the beginning. .h that
10         →       they're already at a disadvantage for doing
11                 well in schoo:l, for making good choices
12                 as they get older in life, .hh an' so: what the
13                 health project is doin' is
```

((4 lines omitted, IE lists some counties that could be compared using County Health Project))

```
17                 .hh an' it allows you to see where you're
18                 doing well, and where you could do better.
19         →       so for example as a- mom eh in my
20                 Anycounty, I took a look at our ranking,
21         →       and you can bet that I uh had a conversation
22         →       with the president of our parent teacher
23                 association to say, .h why don't we have uh
24                 sidewalks and crosswalks. and stoplights
25         →       so that my child can walk safely to school.
26         →       it's a way for her tuh get physical activity,
27         →       it's also a way for her tuh be out in fresh air,
28         →       an' it's a way for her tuh come together with
29                 other parents and other kids,
30   IR:           you [did this? ]
31   IE:   →           [.h so that] she has a sense of
32                 community.
```

In her explanation of the County Health Project tool, the interviewee creates an implicit connection with the local audience through an assertion about the population's shared, local state of affairs: *we have large numbers of kids living in poverty* (lines 06–07). As she unpacks this assertion, we see that it is given as a set of static facts about the local community, as opposed to active struggles within it. First, there is a stark lack of agency in this assertion, in which *child poverty* is something that simply exists, something that *we have*, not something that specific people create or contribute to. This use of *we have ... kids* (line 06), compared to an alternative "*our kids*," also creates an implicit detachment between the addressed community—*we*—and the children under discussion, as if these children are features rather than members of the community (compare also to Extract 2, line 17, *you have parents there and people there*). Finally, these children are stripped of an agentive role as they passively experience the repercussions of their condition, such as *being at a disadvantage* and *having the odds against them*, without actively doing anything to manage, maintain, or overcome that condition. In sum, *children living in poverty* do not appear to be portrayed as an integral part of the local community or as capable of having agency over (their own) health. They are thus implicitly excluded from the audience for which the interviewee designs her message.

The audience is then instantiated by a social category that gives more information about the interviewee's intended recipients. In offering a concrete example of how the County Health Project tool can be used, the interviewee shares her own experience *as a mom* (line 19) talking to *the president of our parent teacher association* (lines 22–23). A few presuppositions in this example need to be unpacked for us to build a better understanding of how the interviewee actively constructs her audience. Quite clearly, this example is designed for the interviewee's fellow parents, more specifically mothers, through her use of the *mom* category. However, the "type" of mother invoked is further defined through the interviewee's reference to a *parent teacher association*. Note that this organization is referred to as one familiar to the audience: The interviewee does not introduce it as an unknown concept that needs to be explained but as a known component—a post-modifier describing the focal institutional category (the organization's *president*). Her use of the possessive pronoun *our* in reference to this organization also relies on the audience's familiarity with the organization—their familiarity with who these organizations typically "belong to" and who the modifier *our* might in this case encompass. The interviewee also introduces her action of talking to the organization's president as presupposed: She frames this action as a response to a question of whether she talked to the president, and she formulates her response as a given, stating *you can bet* on it (line 21). Notice here the added stress on *bet* rather than on either the action of *having a conversation* or on talking specifically to *the president*. The stress placement here seems to further underscore the interviewee's orientation to the action she took as presumed. It is merely her confirmation of that action that needs to be highlighted. Therefore, we can see that the interviewee constructs her audience as not simply being able to relate to *a mom*, but to a mom who is familiar with parent–teacher associations, actively engages in one such association, and treats engagement in this association as commonsensical.

Finally, the health issue that the interviewee brings up in her example adds further specificity to her constructed audience. This issue entails a lack of safe walkways for school children, exemplified in the interviewee's own child not being able to walk safely to school (lines 24–25). This safety issue is formulated as a lack of *sidewalks, crosswalks,* and *stoplights* (line 24), suggesting the interviewee's orientation to a (potentially suburban) environment where potential threats of car accidents, and not of verbal or physical violence to children walking to/from school, appear to be a concern. And the interviewee's solutions to these identified safety issues result in children's increased physical activity and community membership (lines 26–29), rather than in their increased safety from physical or emotional harm. Note also the difference between how the child here is positioned compared to *children in poverty* just prior. Unlike *children in poverty,* the interviewee's child actively engages in various activities, such as walking to school and getting fresh air, and is an integral member of the local community, *coming together with other parents and kids* (lines 28–29 and 31). This contrast not only reinforces the implicit exclusion of *children in poverty* from the local community, but it also more closely illustrates the type of engagement that the interviewee might expect from her audience—their active contribution to the health conditions of those community members that they are directly concerned about. The issue of children living in poverty, while offered as an example of a local health crisis, does not receive a potential solution; instead, a solution is offered for an issue that the audience would arguably more readily relate to, be concerned with, and be able to help with.

Discussion and Conclusion

This chapter has examined how representatives of a U.S. philanthropic foundation construct their audience during media interviews. As these interviews are both informational and promotional in nature, the design of representatives' interview responses can reveal who the foundation aims to inform and engage in their projects. Based on their person references, place references, and activity formulations, foundation representatives appear to be addressing an audience that is part of a united community, shares the foundation's health-related values and concerns, and has the necessary qualifications and attributes to actively address those concerns. The qualifications and attributes in question further suggest that the target audience belongs to the middle class, while those afflicted by poverty are, in contrast, implicitly excluded as recipients of the foundation's messaging.

The construction of the audience as local or national reflects: (1) the foundation's focus on health in states, counties, and cities within the United States and (2) the reach of the local television stations on which the interviews were broadcast. The construction of the audience as a united community is also aligned with the foundation's stated mission of promoting public health by promoting people's sense of community. What's more, positioning their audience as *fellow* members of a local or national community enables the foundation to more directly involve the audience in their mission and to promote their agenda as one that the audience shares. Finally, references to specific personal qualifications and attributes allow the foundation to build the relevance of their agenda for their target viewers—drawing on these viewers' experiences, traits, and abilities to illustrate how they might take part in the foundation's projects.

That the audience also appears to lead a middle-class lifestyle and to espouse corresponding middle-class values deserves further consideration. First, designing their message for this type of audience might reflect the foundation's informed understanding of who the typical viewers of these particular television programs are (based on viewer demographics). Second, references to the concerns and values of this population might be grounded in the foundation sharing these same concerns and values, which it aims to further promote and reinforce as part of its mission, regardless of who their actual audience might be. Third, such a construction of the audience might reflect the foundation's, and more generally society's, underlying ideology that, unlike people living in poverty, the middle class *can* help promote health and, more generally, *can* effect change. Given these possible reasons behind audience construction in our data, several issues would need to be considered as this and other similar organizations strive to communicate their message effectively to their intended viewers.

First, if viewer demographics contribute to institutional representatives referencing specific experiences and attributes in their messaging, it would be important to examine: (1) to what extent the referenced experiences and attributes authentically represent those of the actual audience, (2) whether concerned members of other demographic characteristics are included in the messaging through other outlets, and (3) whether representatives effectively and appropriately adjust the referenced experiences and attributes according to their audience. In the case of the foundation in our data, we wonder whether all the (potentially) concerned community members were in fact reached via these interviews. Given that this foundation aimed to create a sense of community and to engage groups and individuals not traditionally seen as shaping public health, we would expect a more diverse audience to be targeted by the foundation's messaging. Throughout our data, however, representatives quite consistently illustrated the foundation's concerns and objectives by drawing on experiences of middle-class professionals with children. It would be worth exploring if by incorporating more diverse social categories, concerns, and capabilities in their messaging, the foundation might engage more diverse members of the local community in their projects.

Second, if organizations draw on specific categories and activities in their messaging because those categories and activities best reflect their own values and objectives, it is worth examining whether those who *should* be informed are in fact the ones being informed. In other words, if an organization wishes to promote its work more widely, it should go beyond solely addressing an audience that already shares its goals and concerns. Finding the avenues to reach an audience with significantly different concerns, values, or experiences and identifying ways to build a connection with and engage such a "distant" audience could help organizations promote their agenda and increase their overall impact. And when those who should be informed are already recognized as being at risk and vulnerable, the impetus for addressing the most affected, even if socioculturally more distant, audience is even greater.

Finally, exploring how underlying ideologies might shape who is addressed, how, and why can uncover the implicit, ingrained, even hidden values not only of particular organizations but of society in general. Close examination of a philanthropic organization's messaging might thus reveal a paradox between their proclaimed mission and their implicit ideology. For instance, while an organization might strive to engage non-traditional actors in their projects, promote equity, and build tight-knit communities so as to promote social change, their messaging might imply something quite different: (1) In attempting to engage non-traditional actors, organizations might inadvertently ascribe agency to the socially dominant (the middle class) but take it away from the disenfranchised (the poor); (2) in attempting to promote equity, organizations might end up addressing the social concerns of the dominant but not those of the disenfranchised; and (3) in attempting to create a community, organizations might manage to build connections with the dominant but create distance from the disenfranchised. We see this potential paradox as rooted in larger social ideologies and only tacitly evidenced in institutional representatives' subtle language choices. Nevertheless, very subtle language choices can have quite significant interactional consequences. Making these choices carefully and purposefully could allow philanthropic organizations to communicate much more genuinely with their audiences and to effectively involve all those concerned in their messaging.

References

Armon, R. (2016). Expert positions and scientific contexts: Storying research in the news media. *Discourse & Communication, 10*(1), 3–21.

Clayman, S. E. (1989). The production of punctuality: Social interaction, temporal organization, and social structure. *American Journal of Sociology, 95*(3), 659–691.

Clayman, S. E. (2002). Tribune of the people: Maintaining the legitimacy of aggressive journalism. *Media, Culture & Society, 24*(2), 191–210.

Clayman, S. E. (2010). Questioning in broadcast journalism. In A. F. Freed & S. Ehrlich (Eds.), *"Why do you ask?": The function of questions in institutional discourse* (pp. 256–278). Oxford: Oxford University Press.

Clayman, S. E. (2013). Conversation analysis in the news interview. In J. Sidnell & T. Stivers (Eds.), *The handbook of conversation analysis* (pp. 630–656). Malden, MA: Blackwell Publishing.

Clayman, S. E. (2015). Broadcast talk. In W. Donsbach (Ed.), *Concise encyclopedia of communication* (p. 51). Oxford: Wiley-Blackwell.

Clayman, S. E., & Heritage, J. (2002). *The news interview: Journalists and public figures on the air*. Cambridge: Cambridge University Press.

Data USA (n.d.). Retrieved from https://datausa.io/ (accessed November 15, 2018).

Goffman, E. (1981). *Forms of talk*. Philadelphia, PA: University of Pennsylvania Press.

Heritage, J. (1985). Analyzing news interviews: Aspects of the production of talk for an overhearing audience. In T. van Dijk (Ed.), *Handbook of discourse analysis* (Vol. 3, pp. 95–117). New York: Academic Press.

Tilney, M. (2015). Keeping the upper-hand: Pragmatic techniques in the media interview. *Critical Approaches to Discourse Analysis across Disciplines, 7*(2), 180–199.

Part Three

Managing Logistics

But-prefacing for Refocusing in Public Talk

Ann Tai Choe and Elizabeth Reddington
*University of Hawai'i at Mānoa and
Teachers College, Columbia University*

Introduction

In this chapter, we examine a little word that appears to do big work (Bolden, 2006) in public discourse. Syntactically, the English *but* is a coordinating conjunction that combines two constituents belonging to equal categories (Carnie, 2013). It can be used to mark a contrastive relation (as in, *Mary is strict, but John is easy-going*) (Fraser, 1996; Halliday & Hasan, 1976), an adversative relation (as in, *John is handsome, but he doesn't have great charisma*) (Halliday & Hasan, 1976), and, somewhat relatedly, a denial of expectations (as in, *She is not a painter, but she is an artist*) (Blakemore, 1989, 2000, 2002; Lakoff, 1971) or a cancellation (as in, *I don't like those paintings very much, but I find them unforgettable*) (Bell, 1998). It can also serve as a mitigating device that modifies a message which may appear "disadvantageous to the addressee" (as in, *I see your point, but ...*) (Fraser, 1996, p. 184). These studies have shown that *but* can take on various semantic functions in discourse (see also Fraser, 2008, 2009, 2013); however, because the examples in these studies tend to be shown isolated from a larger context (for an exception, see Schiffrin, 1987), the sequential function of *but* in naturally occurring interaction remains an area worthy of further investigation.

In the conversation analysis (CA) literature, discourse markers—such as *and, or, so,* and *but,* inter alia—can be described as little words that accomplish big interactional tasks in discourse (Bolden, 2006). Waring (2003) defines discourse markers as "words or expressions that rise above their semantic/referential meanings to take on complex interactional duties" (p. 416). Within the past few decades, a growing number of CA scholars have investigated what these interactional duties might be across different contexts. Examples of such work include, but are not limited to, Heritage's (1984) work on *oh* as a change-of-state token in natural conversation; Schegloff and Lerner's (2009) work on *well* in turn-initial position for indicating non-straightforwardness in responding to *wh*-questions; Bolden's (2006, 2009) work on *so*-prefacing for marking other-attentive topics; Drake's (2015) work on turn-final *or* for indexing uncertainty in polar questions; Park's (2010) study on *anyway* as a sequence-ending device; and Waring's (2012) study on *now*-prefacing in managing disaffiliation. In this study, we examine a special function of *but* in public events that involve a ratified, overhearing audience (Goffman, 1981)—a context in which speakers are accountable for producing talk or actions that are relevant to all parties.

As such, we also build on Schiffrin's (1987) seminal work on *but* as a discourse marker used by English speakers in question-answer sequences. Based on a collection of sociolinguistic interview data, Schiffrin found that *but* can be used by a speaker to recover a point that had been misunderstood, challenged, and/or interrupted (as in, *But anyway, my point is* …). She argues that, besides contrasting ideas, *but* can sometimes express "the referential contrast marked by *however* and the functional contrast marked by *anyway*" (p. 165). Expanding on Schiffrin's (1987) finding that *but* can signal not only contrasting ideas but also contrasting actions, the focus of our study is to investigate *but*-prefacing as an interactional practice in communicating with the public.

Data

Our data come from a corpus of audio- and/or video-recorded naturally occurring interactions involving representatives of a philanthropic foundation. Specifically, we examined the recordings and transcripts of fifty-eight public events, including Q&A sessions following eighteen public talks and panel discussions, Q&A sessions following twenty-five webinars, nine podcast interviews, and six television interviews.

While initially engaged in unmotivated looking (Psathas, 1995), we noticed a recurring phenomenon in the data in which *but* appeared to do more than mark a contrastive idea or an unexpected proposition. To better illustrate this phenomenon, consider the use of *but* by the podcast interviewee (IE) in lines 08 and 20 below.

(1) but we can build

```
01   IE:         and- (0.2) .hh and so we:: take that very
02               seriously. a:::nd try to (0.2) .hh
03               >characterize< what ↑are the potential side
04               effects.
05   IR:         mhm?
06   IE:         we tend to think that they're gonna be lower
07               than things like pharmaceuticals?=and small
08     →         molecules? but (0.2) .hh it's reasonable to
09               say that there ↑might be side effects=and so
10               we think about that a lot. ((continues))
```

((lines 11–18 omitted))

```
19   IE:         .hh the ↑cool thing, and this is a longer
20     →         conversation.=but (0.3) we can bui::ld (.)
21               these checks into our game. (0.2) .hh so
22               we're doing a study on a video game now
23               that we developed in our lab ((continues))
```

In discussing the potential side effects of video games on cognitive development, the interviewee states that, compared to pharmaceutical drugs, video games presumably have *lower* side effects (line 06). In line 08, the IE uses *but* to mark an adversarial relationship between what has been stated and what comes next: Despite the fact that playing video games may have less serious side effects than taking medication, it is reasonable to be thinking about what the side effects might be (lines 06–10).

In the lines omitted, the IE identifies overplaying as a well-recognized side effect of video games. As he is about to introduce a solution, or *the cool thing* in line 19, he adds the evaluative comment, *and this is a longer conversation*. Immediately after, he uses *but* to begin a new turn-constructional unit (TCU) and present the solution of building *checks* into the game (lines 20–21). Unlike its counterpart in line 08, the function of *but* here is less straightforward; it does not seem to mark a contrastive or adversative relation between two propositions—so, we began to wonder, what is it doing here?

We proceeded to build a collection that ultimately consisted of seventy-nine segments of talk in which such *but*-prefaced utterances occurred. Guided by CA's principal analytic question, "why that now?" (Schegloff & Sacks, 1973), we closely examined the sequential environments of *but* through line-by-line analysis. In what follows, we will show how speakers leverage the contrastive nature of *but* to regain the focus of a projected action or an action in-progress following some sort of deviation from the main business of the talk.

Analysis and Findings

In this section, we will present cases[1] where *but* appears in TCU-initial position as speakers turn or return to the primary interactional agenda of doing questioning, commenting, responding, or moderating in public discourse. Specifically, we will show how *but*-prefacing is employed by speakers to resume the main business following talk that can be heard as (1) attending to ancillary matters, (2) attending to procedural matters, or (3) managing expectations. We refer to these as *self-initiated* divergences in that it is the current speaker who delays or interrupts the expected action. The section will end with a unique case of *but*-prefacing deployed in response to an *other-initiated* divergence. We argue that *but* functions as a refocusing device in these environments; in other words, it helps speakers transition from talk that departs from the main agenda to pursue the expected course of action.

But-prefacing to Shift from Ancillary Matters to Main Business

But-prefacing may be used by a speaker after talk that can be characterized as ancillary to the main business of the turn. As will be shown, attending to "ancillary matters" may involve providing details or background information on the developing question or response or implementing other actions that, temporarily, deviate from the expected action or action in-progress. Extract 2 comes from a face-to-face Q&A session following a moderated panel discussion sponsored by the foundation that centered on using data for health. After being nominated by the moderator (MO), the audience member (AU) introduces herself, but instead of immediately launching the question, she provides additional background to contextualize it.

(2) but curious

```
01    AU:           uh B↑rooke Johnson with the Trust for
02                  Health La::nd,=a director (.) Na:tional IEC
03                  and planning efforts.=and (0.2) ↑curious so
04                  you know we're talking a lot about ↑how
05                  do we keep this data updated. >you know<
06                  it's great that we ha:ve, it's great that
07                  we're compiling it,=we're creating it.
08                  (0.3)
09    AU:    →      .hhh but ↑curi::ous u::m (0.2) .hh what you
10                  think about cro:wdsourcing. <and if not (.)
11                  com↑pletely opening up, uh enriching and
12                  enhancing,=and (0.2) .hh keeping our data
13                  up to date, (0.2) through crowdsourcing
14                  maybe through something li:ke a version
15                  of citizen scientist? that ca:n enhance our
16                  data?=maybe there are public health.
17           →      ↓citizen scientists (0.2) but- curious if
18                  you've ha::d um any (0.2) experience with (.)
19                  °uh° enriching your data and keeping your
20                  data up to date in that way?=and what you
21                  ↑think about that.
22                  ((PAs gaze to each other))-(7.2)
```

In line 03, AU expresses that she is *curious* about something, which is perhaps the start of a question. Rather than reveal the object of her curiosity, in lines 03–05, she begins a new TCU with *so* and references the topic of the panel discussion—how to keep data updated. She then offers positive assessments of current efforts to compile and create data (lines 06–07). Following the 0.3-second gap and a deep inbreath, in lines 09–10, she finally produces the question in a new TCU prefaced by *but but curious um (0.2) .hh what you think about crowdsourcing*. On one level, *but* may be heard as suggesting a contrast between what is done (i.e., current efforts) and what could be done (i.e., crowdsourcing). Yet it also marks another sort of contrast—between the previous action of providing background information and that of asking the question. By thus drawing a line between background information and the question itself, and by recycling the word *curious*, the questioner directs listeners' focus back to the main business of the turn.

Before handing the floor over to the panelists, AU offers a vision of how crowdsourcing could be manifested, potentially with the help of citizen scientists (lines 10–17). Having made this proposal, in line 17, she once again uses *but*-prefacing, in conjunction with repetition of the word *curious*, to regain focus. As seen in the subsequent lines (lines 17–21), she offers another formulation of the question with some elaboration on the concept of crowdsourcing and closes the turn by repeating part of her original question: *but curious ... what you think about* X. By prefacing the final formulation of the question with *but*, AU marks a contrast between immediately preceding talk and the final question, treating the former as ancillary and the latter as the main business. In this way, the question is rendered salient for the panelists and other audience members.

The following two examples show instances in which *but*-prefacing occurs after a speaker produces talk that deviates from the expected course of action. Extract 3 comes from a face-to-face Q&A session following a foundation representative's (PR) presentation, which focused on promoting a new strategy for improving population health. The extract begins with the moderator inviting AU to ask a question. After his self-introduction, instead of asking a question, AU delivers a humorous remark.

(3) but learning about health-based social movements

```
01    MO:         ((leaning toward mic))-next. [next question.]
02    AU:                                      [hey,           ]
03                hi Doctor Powell, thanks for being here. uh
04                my name is Jayden Miller, I'm a first #yea:r#
05                (0.2) MPH student #i::n# the: Department of
06                Sociomedical Science, #u:h,# (0.3) I've been
07                at Anyschool for a w:↑ee:k, s:o [naturally I
08                                                [((light laughter
```

```
09                          from audience))
10      AU:                 am an- I'm an expert on (.) health based
11                          social move[ments now. ((smiles?))
12                                      [((laughter from audience))
13      PR:                         [>that's g[reat.<
14      AU:    →                              [but uh,
15      PR:                 [lay- lay it on me.
16      AU:                 [(((leans back from mic, smiling, laughing?))
17                          [((laughter from audience))
18      PR?:                [↑HHEH HHEH HEH
19                          [((laughter from audience))
20      AU:                 ((talking over fading laughter))-u::m,
21                          [(((touches chest))-so if you need tuh talk
22      PR?:                [↑UH HE-
23      AU:                 ((taps fingers to chest))-tuh me,
24                          ((quick head turn to side))-°y'know.° (.h)
25                          [uh:,   ]
26      PR?:                [HHH]
27      AU:    →            .TCH. bu:t, (0.2) {(((gestures to PR))-learning
28                          about} health based social movements, (.)
29                          u:h they arise from a grassroots level of
30                          people who share a a condition and who
31                          sha:re (0.3) a life history, ((continues))
```

In lines 03–06, AU greets the foundation representative and introduces himself—a common practice that is found throughout our data involving post-presentation Q&A sessions (see also Extracts 2 and 4, and Clemente, this volume). Following the self-introduction, where AU might be expected to launch a question, he instead announces that he has been at school for a week and makes an ironic evaluation of his background: *so naturally ... I'm an expert on (.) health based social movements now* (lines 6–7 and 10–11). The self-evaluation is treated by other participants as humorous, as evidenced by the audience's laughter (line 12) and PR's positive assessment, *that's great* (line 13), which may be heard as similarly playful.

In overlap with the positive assessment, AU makes his first attempt to continue current speakership and focus on questioning through *but*-prefacing (line 14); however, this is quickly abandoned as PR extends the playful frame by adding *lay it on me* (line 15), indicating his readiness to take up the challenge. Following laughter from the audience, in line 20, where AU might again be expected to produce a question, he instead extends the playful sequence by ironically inverting the expert-novice status of the presenter and himself: He touches his chest while offering PR an opportunity to seek consultation from him (lines 20–21 and 23–25). Thus far, the main business of questioning has been delayed due to the participants' collaborative engagement in humor talk.

After the laughter audible in line 26, AU produces a click (.*TCH*) in line 27. By prefacing the next TCU with *but*, he signals a contrast between his prior actions and what he will do next: provide background and ask a question. He pauses briefly before reintroducing the topic of the question, originally referenced in his first humorous remark: *but (0.2) learning about health based social movements*. AU further underscores the shift in focus by gesturing toward PR as he begins to provide background (partially shown in lines 27–31). In this case, then, we see a speaker using *but*-prefacing to get his questioning turn "back on track" following his initiation of humor talk.

The final example in this section shows another case in which an audience member employs *but*-prefacing to return to the expected action of doing questioning. AU is selected to ask a question after a panelist (PA1) responds to the audience question on crowdsourcing (Extract 2). Although a question is produced early in the turn (lines 03–06), AU proceeds with further details to support the question and initiates a topical digression to correct a mistake in PA1's prior talk.

(4) but policy advocacy

```
01    AU:        ↑somewhat related question, I'::m Lawrence
02               Robins?=from Anyinstitute. thank you,=
03               ↑a:ll of you. (0.2) .hh I'm wondering i:f you
04               ca:n either already see or project the ↑u:ses
05               of these data fo:r (0.2) policy advocacy and
06               change. (0.2) a ↑couple of us >uh< perhaps
07               at the state legislative, (0.2) level?=because

      ((lines 08-21 omitted))

22               the nuances.< (0.2) .hh it seems like the
23               public S↑I:de of this at a Lo::t of different
```

24		levels, (0.2) is wide open?=and has
25		tremendous po↑tential.=it may be too early=
26	→	but (0.2) .hh u:m <be interested in what you
27		kno::w, .h about that. and I'm >very
28		familiar with RoadWide< by the way?=
29		°and-° [.hh
30	PA1:	[(((*gazes to AU and nods*))-°mhm?°
31	AU:	u::h- (0.2) <it's Anyuniversity actually?=
32		[(if) you're on (tweet.)
33	PA1:	[(((*gazes to AU and nods*))-°thank you.°
34		(0.2)
35	AU:	[(e-con). and a group called] C E=
36	PA1:	[°yep. thank you.°]
37	AU:	=<if anyone's interested it ↑i:s a
38		crowdsourcing (0.2) .hh uh platform for
39		exactly what (0.4) you were saying.
40		(0.5)
41	AU: →	but (.) policy advocacy::, (0.2) local
42		accountability? .tsk
43		(1.8)
44	PA2:	°↑this is a >sort of sort of<° general
45		response to tha:t ((*continues*))

After introducing himself and showing appreciation to the panelists, in the next TCU, AU launches a question regarding policy advocacy and change: *I'm wondering if you can either already see or project the uses of these data for (0.2) policy advocacy and change* (lines 03–06). Although the main business of the turn has ostensibly been accomplished, AU continues to elaborate and contextualize the question (beginning in line 07, partially shown), pointing out a potential gap in current efforts to use data for public health and then attributing it to lack of investment in local neighborhoods.

In lines 22–25, AU provides an upshot and produces an abbreviated version of his question: *but (0.2) .hh um be interested in what you know .h about that* (lines 26–27)—marking the shift from background to question with *but*. Following the pitch drop at the end of the TCU, where AU might be expected to relinquish the floor, he instead continues current speakership by claiming familiarity with a referent mentioned in PA1's prior talk. The use of the disjunctive marker *by the way* (line 28) at the end of the TCU suggests a topic shift (Crow, 1983). AU then provides a correction of the referent, which is both acknowledged and accepted by PA1 (lines 33 and 36). Thus far, AU has extended the questioning turn by providing ancillary details to his question and shifting the topic to correct a mistake made by PA1. Although the question has already been stated, the panelists are not yet given a turn to respond.

Following a 0.5-second gap in line 40, AU uses *but* to launch a new TCU, during which he offers a short version of the question (lines 41–42), similar in wording to the original question at the beginning of the turn, before finally relinquishing the floor. The use of *but*-prefacing again serves to highlight a shift between what has been done and what will come next, foregrounding the question for the benefit of the panelists who must respond and for the overhearing audience.

Altogether, the extracts above show how *but*-prefacing is used by speakers to resume the main business after producing talk that addresses ancillary matters. The deviations can be caused by the speaker's agency to expand on the details of a question in-progress (Extract 2), employ humor (Extract 3), or initiate a topic shift (Extract 4). In all cases, *but* is used to mark a contrast between what came before (i.e., ancillary matters) and what comes next (i.e., main business), and it instructs listeners to hear what comes next as what matters most.

But-prefacing to Shift from Procedural Matters to Main Business

The extracts in this section will show a slightly different environment in which *but*-prefacing can occur. Specifically, we will show that it can occur when there is a need to resume the main business following an interruption to address procedural matters—for example, talk that addresses the organization of the activity or deals with contingencies that might affect progressivity. Extract 5 comes from a face-to-face Q&A session following a moderated panel discussion with two invited speakers: a foundation representative and a representative of a food and beverage industry company. The extract begins with the moderator projecting her own upcoming question to the speakers.

(5) but what is your vision

```
01    MO:           .hh (.) ↑what is- op- {((gazes down to paper))-
02                  I wanna ask the both of} you.={((gazes and
03                  palm towards AU))-and again >we're gonna
04                  be} {((gazes down at paper))-taking questions
05    →             from the audience in a minute.<}=but .hhh
06                  (.) ↑what is your <vision> of what .hh (0.4)
07                  u::h healthy::, (.) u-u-u::h <foo::d> u::m (.)
08                  and beverage choices should be:.
```

In lines 01–02, MO begins to ask a question to the panelists (*what is-*) but then quickly repairs it with a pre-pre (Scheglo ff, 1980): *I wanna ask the both of you*. At the same time, she gazes down to her paper (lines 01–02), possibly using it as a reminder of her question. In so doing, MO projects that a question is forthcoming.

What comes next is still not the question, however. Beginning in line 02, MO shifts her gaze to the audience and extends her palm toward them as she launches a new TCU. Through latching, she prefaces the new TCU with *and again*, and then states in quicker speech: *we're gonna be taking questions from the audience in a minute*, shifting her gaze back to the paper (lines 02–05). In contrast to the preceding TCU (lines 01–02), where MO addressed the panelists as her primary addressees, the message in this turn is directed toward all audience members. Specifically, the moderator informs the audience about the organization of the ongoing activity—that is, the moderator will invite questions from the audience after she delivers hers. Having made the announcement about future procedures for taking questions, in line 05, she begins a new TCU through a latched *but* and a deep inbreath. After a micropause, MO finally launches her question, once again orienting to the panelists as the primary recipients: *what is your vision of what ... healthy ... food um and beverage choices should be* (lines 06–08). By prefacing the next TCU with *but*, MO marks the end of prior talk that deals with procedural matters and resumes the main action of questioning.

Our next two examples show instances in which *but*-prefacing is used to regain focus following talk that deals with contingencies that may affect the progressivity of the interaction. Extract 6 comes from the beginning of a face-to-face Q&A session following individual presentations by a group of panelists at an event sponsored by the foundation. The moderator initiates a debriefing of the presentations (lines 01–03) but encounters a technical difficulty.

(6) but I wanted to talk about

```
01    MO:         w- hh we've had some great u:m (0.2)
02                opportunities with our ((holds and gazes to
03                tablet))-speakers today. and I <just lost my>
04                um-
05                ((smiles and then shows tablet with blank screen))-
06                (1.2)
07                .hhh (0.2) ((gazes down))-h(hh) I just lost
08    →           my screen.={(((shifts gaze to AU))-but I wanted
09                to:, .hh I wanted to} (.) talk a little bit about
10                what we heard today. it's really interesting-
11                we started out with Eva ((continues))
```

As MO completes her transitional remark with the assessment, *we've had some great um (0.2) opportunities with our speakers today* (lines 01–03), she reaches for a tablet and gazes to it. Her bodily orientation toward the device at this moment suggests its relevance as a tool for carrying out the Q&A session. Instead of continuing the transitional remark or formulating a question, as might be expected, in lines 03–04, MO reports a technical difficulty that she is currently facing: *and I just lost my um-*.

Within the 1.2-second gap (lines 05–06), MO smiles and displays the blank screen to the audience, accounting for the suspension of her original course of action—that is, to debrief and transition into the Q&A session. In lines 07–08, she gazes down while verbalizing the problem: *h(hh) (0.2) I just lost my screen*. In lines 08–10, however, MO quickly launches a new TCU through a latched *but* while shifting her gaze toward the audience: *but I wanted to ... talk a little bit about what we heard today*. *But* here marks a contrast between talk that makes public the technical difficulty and the resumption of main business. Specifically, it helps MO to return to the agenda she set out to accomplish before the interruption (note also the use of past tense, *wanted to*). As seen in lines 09 to 11, she resumes the original course of action, offering a debrief of the presentations (partially shown).

Our last example in this section comes from a Q&A session following a webinar presentation, which focused on promoting a scholarship program offered by the foundation. The moderator, who is also a foundation representative, reads an audience member contribution and begins responding (lines 02–08); however, her response in-progress is interrupted as she attends to a potential technical difficulty.

(7) but our understanding is

```
01    MO:           <well the NEXt QUEstion? i:::s the:: uh (0.2)
02                  {((reading voice))-<I believe B dash L is- Better
03                  Living focuses on how health disparities?
04                  <within the U.S.? (0.2) but development of
05                  solutions might be best demonstrated in less
06                  developed countries.} (0.2) °um.° OUr
07                  understanding of this is,=this is a:: (.)
08                  domestic U.S. and territor(ies) (.) program.
09                  (0.2) I would <also ask> Daniel Long to::
10                  ring ↑in on that either by chat? (0.2) O:::r
11                  I be↑lieve that um Daniel is muted. so::. if
12                  JOey, our host, could >↑unmute Daniel.=
13                  that might be helpful<=↑or Daniel,=please
14                  feel free to chat i:::n. (0.2) um the:: answer
15      →           to that. <but OUr understanding is this is
16                  U.S. ↑a::nd (.) >and territories.<=so:: (.) >not
17                  an international< program.
```

It is worth noting that the audience member "question" also includes a mitigated proposal: The first TCU seeks confirmation of the foundation's U.S. focus and contrasts with the following assertion that *development of solutions might be best demonstrated in less developed countries* (note the use of *but* to contrast the two propositions) (lines 02–06). After voicing the question/comment on behalf of the audience (see King, this volume), MO provides a short response. The response can also be heard as somewhat mitigated: The quiet filler (*um*) and the response preface *our understanding of this is* (lines 06–07) imply a degree of uncertainty. Following a brief pause, she invites a colleague, Daniel, to comment on the subject matter (lines 09–10).

Despite the signal for Daniel to take the floor, after a 0.2-second gap, MO launches a new TCU through an elongated *or* (line 10) and makes public a potential technical difficulty—that is, Daniel's line is muted (line 11). She then addresses talk to Joey, the host of the webinar, to resolve the technical issue (lines 11–13). It is interesting to note that, within this turn, MO gives instructions to the host of the webinar but addresses him and his affiliation in the third person: *so if Joey, our host, could unmute Daniel* (lines 11–13), thus simultaneously orienting to the overhearing audience as a recipient of the talk. Without giving up the floor, however, MO offers another alternative solution through latching and raised pitch on *or*, re-inviting Daniel to contribute his version of the response by typing or chatting it in (lines 13–15).

Following the falling intonation on *that* in line 15, which terminates the previous TCU, MO secures the next TCU through *but*-prefacing in a rush-through, during which she reiterates her response with some expansion: *but our understanding is* (lines 15–17). By prefacing the new TCU with *but*, she marks a shift from talk that attends to procedural matters to the original course of action (i.e., answering the question). The use of *but* in line 15 helps MO to return to the response-in-progress and redirects all listeners' attention back to the main focus at hand.

In sum, the extracts presented in this section have shown how *but* is used at the beginning of a new TCU following an interruption to address procedural matters. These interruptions may include talk that attends to the organization of the activity (Extract 5) or manages contingencies that affect the progressivity of talk (Extracts 6 and 7). In contrast to the previous section, where we illustrated the use of *but*-prefacing to mark a contrast between ancillary matters and main business, the examples included in this section include talk that is more interruptive in that it is unrelated to the topic underway. Like the previous section, however, this section has also shown that *but* in TCU-initial position can signal a transition between a prior action and the subsequent action, which is the action that matters most for the recipients.

But-prefacing to Shift from Expectation Management to Main Business

Speakers may also digress to offer accounts related to their ability to complete the projected or in-progress action or to produce evaluations of their own prior or upcoming talk. Following such efforts to manage recipient and audience expectations, participants routinely employ *but*-prefacing to mark a shift in focus as they begin or resume the main business of the turn.

Extract 8 comes from a webinar hosted by the foundation for prospective grant applicants. In lines 01–06, the moderator introduces the topic of the question (*a question regarding IRB* [Institutional Review Board] *and surveys*) and proceeds to read the typed-in question, which can be summarized as, *do all projects require university IRB approval*? An answer to this question is called for in the presenter's (PR) next turn. However, it appears that the presenter cannot provide a straightforward *yes* or *no*.

(8) but I will tell you

```
01    MO:           thank you. here's a question regarding IRB
02                  and surveys. u:m ((reading voice))-as long as the
03                  survey procedures comply with national
04                  ethics standards outlined in the guidelines
05                  do all proposed projects have to: be
06                  approved by university IRB committee?
07                  (1.0)
08    PR:           .HHH ((click)) good- good question I think
09                  u::m and I'm not u:h I am not an attorney, u:h
10        →         but I will tell you uhm I think th- you know
11                  the requirements about IRBs (the) IRB
12                  requirements uhm are- are- duh are-
13                  conditioned first and foremost based on the
14                  the organization u::h that <houses> uh: the
15                  team that is conducting uh the study. ((continues))
```

While gaps between questions and answers, such as that seen in line 07, are not uncommon in these webinars (speakers may need to negotiate who will answer or unmute lines), there are other indicators that the response will not be straightforward, including the big inbreath with which the presenter begins his turn in line 08. Following his positive assessment of the question, the presenter may be starting to offer a hedged answer with *I think*. However, he abandons this trajectory and begins another with the connective marker *and*, ultimately, completing the TCU with: *I am not an attorney* (line 09). He has, for the moment, put off the task of answering to invoke a professional category of which he is not a member. Formatted as an extension of prior talk, this assertion is designed to be heard as relevant. In fact, it becomes a comment on the representative's ability to respond to the question. The questioner and the rest of the audience are instructed to hear the answer as limited given that the respondent is not able to provide a legal perspective.

Following slight hesitation, the presenter begins a new TCU with *but*, followed by *I will tell you* (line 10). With *but*, the speaker implies a contrast between what he will not or cannot tell (i.e., he cannot provide a legal answer) and what he *will tell,* signaling a return to answering. After slight hesitation, he proceeds to recycle the *I think* with which he initially began his answer and note that IRB requirements are determined by the organization *that houses* the research team (lines 10–15). After elaborating on this point, he completes the response not with a *yes* or *no* but by advising the questioner to check the requirements at their institution (not shown).

In brief, the TCU *and I am not an attorney* offers a comment on the speaker's ability to answer the question and instructs participants to hear what comes next as an answer from a non-legal perspective. With this disclaimer made, the speaker continues answering, marking the resumption of the main business with *but*.

Speakers also work to manage expectations even before the expected action has gotten underway. The following extract comes from another foundation webinar for prospective grant applicants. In lines 01–05, the moderator selects two possible respondents before repeating an audience member question, which asks for examples of *the types of health effects on business* that the foundation is interested in. (The 2-second gap that precedes the response may be reflective of negotiation between the representatives regarding who should respond and/or of something problematic about the question.)

(9) but in kind of this second category
```
01    MO:        Molly ((PR)) or Martha you may >wanna take
02               that one<. =>again.< (.) ((reading voice))-<can you
03               provide some examples of the types (.) of
04               health effects on bu̱siness, (.) that you're
05               hoping to see propo::sed.
06               (2.0)
07    PR:        so::, I'm- I'm not exactly su::re what is
```

```
08    →         meant by: health effects.=but um i::n >kind
09                  of this< (.) ↑second category of major topics
10                  in the call for proposal, (0.2) .hh uh one thing
11                  we're interested th↑E:re >is kind of< the
12                  interplay between the health of the community,
13                  market factors, and a business's viability::,
14                  ((continues))
```

Following the gap in line 06, one of the nominated presenters launches a turn with an elongated *so*, which may indicate the non-straightforward nature of the response to come (line 07). Rather than answering by providing the requested examples, after a cutoff on *I'm*, the presenter states that she is *not exactly sure what is meant by health effects* (lines 07–08), indicating a possible problem with understanding a term that is central to the question. As the format of these webinars does not allow for back-and-forth between presenters and audience members, the presenter does not actually have the opportunity to seek and receive clarification. By making the understanding problem public, she pre-emptively offers an account for what may turn out to be, for the questioner, an incomplete or ill-fitted response. She then moves quickly on to answering: With a latch, she begins a new TCU with *but* (line 08), refers to the call for proposals that is available, and identifies some topics that are of interest to the foundation (partially shown in lines 08–14). With the use of *but*, she treats her own prior talk as "not the main point," and turns to the business of answering, as best she can under the circumstances.

While Extracts 8 and 9 illustrate cases in which speakers interrupt or delay the action called for to offer information that downplays the speaker's ability to answer, *but*-prefacing can occur after other kinds of expectation management work, where speakers diverge from the action projected, or already underway, to offer evaluations of their own talk.

The following extract comes from the Q&A portion of a moderated panel discussion on the topic of data and health, held in front of a live audience (see also Extracts 2–4). As the extract begins, the moderator is responding (lines 01–08) to an audience member comment (not shown) about the futility of continuing to collect data when it does not appear to have made an impact on health disparities. In line 09, a panelist self-selects and offers a response of his own.

(10) but there was a thing that broke out

```
01   MO:          for themselves. necessarily and I think- we
02                wanna continue and make sure that we-
03                continue that conversation .h um and call
04                people to the carpet and call people to
05                action call business call academia .h call
06                health systems to action .h for those people
07                who come into their d- their doors and those
08                people who don't. .h [so.  ]
09   PA:                               [s- y-]
10                just an anecdote which I think is- kind of
11                fascinating (an-) you- you can- look this up
12   →            but there was a (.) th↑ing that broke out in the
13                Anycity school district (.) last year where (.) there's
14                a big grant to provide (.) uh ipa:ds or some
15                kind of computer (.) computing in the school,
16                ((continues))
```

In line 09, the panelist launches his turn with cutoffs, before offering a characterization of the talk to come as *just an anecdote* which is *kind of fascinating* (lines 10–11). The talk to come is not, therefore, framed as an answer or a challenge to the audience member's or moderator's perspective but rather as a related story. While its import may be downplayed through the use of *just* and the choice of *anecdote*, rather than *story*, as a label, the speaker also takes steps to highlight other aspects of the upcoming telling: He assesses it positively not only as *kind of fascinating* but also as true (*you can look this up*) (lines 10–11). Following these prefatory evaluations, the speaker then launches a new TCU with *but* that offers setting information (*Anycity school district (.) last year*) and launches the telling (lines 12–15). The telling can be heard as responding to, and ultimately affirming, the audience member's point that technology itself is not a solution to all public health issues (not shown).

Thus, before beginning the main business of the responding turn, the speaker provides a preview that instructs listeners to hear what comes next as both relevant and interesting. *But* signals the end of the prefatory comments and highlights the "official launch" of the story itself.

In this section, we have shown cases in which *but*-prefacing is deployed following talk geared toward a particular action, specifically, managing recipient/audience expectations regarding the nature of the turn and what it will accomplish. Such talk may function as a disclaimer regarding the speaker's ability to thoroughly complete the expected action (Extracts 8 and 9) or evaluate the content of the turn and offer instructions on how to hear it (Extract 10). In all cases, *but* marks the beginning or resumption of the main business.

But-prefacing to Shift from Another Speaker's Agenda

In the cases discussed thus far, *but*-prefacing occurs as a response to self-initiated divergences from the projected or in-progress action. In other words, it is the current speaker who diverges and then focuses, or refocuses, on the main business. In only a handful of cases in our data is *but*-prefacing used for refocusing in response to a co-participant's action.

Extract 11 offers an example of these relatively rare circumstances. It comes from the beginning of a televised interview with a leader of the foundation, as the interviewer (IR) is revealing aspects of the interviewee's (IE) background for the audience.

```
(11) but what it talks about here is
     01   IR:         not everyone who leads a .hh foundation
     02               has the background you have.=
     03   IE:         =uh,=
     04   IR:         =you're ((shakes head))-a practicing physician?
     05   IE:         [    ((nods))   ]
     06   IR:         [fo:r (.) a few yea]rs?
     07   IE:         >op-< we don't need to talk about how
     08               many, [yeah? huh huh huh]
     09   IR:               [{((raises eyebrows))->°oh°< I'm just
     10               sayi:ng} you have     ] ((flips through foundation
     11   →           report))-an impressive background.=.hh but
     12               what it- what it talks about here is, .hh it breaks
     13               do:wn (.) you know in- in the: foundation report.
     14               what this Framework for Health really is and it
     15               breaks it down in a way that (.) is real for people.=
     16               =and I want you to help us with this. ((continues))
```

In lines 04 and 06, the interviewer notes that the interviewee is a *practicing physician* and has been *for a few years*. The formulation *a few years* highlights the extensiveness of the interviewee's experience while mitigating what this implies about her age—a personal and potentially delicate topic in public discussion. The interviewee nods *yes* in line 05, confirming the first fact (*practicing physician*) as the interviewer adds the increment *for a few years*. In lines 07 and 08, rather than offer another aligning response (i.e., another confirmation), she responds to the increment with: *we don't need to talk about how many*. The clausal response problematizes the question, casting "number of years in the profession" as a topic that does not require further specification or as one that may not be appropriate. The interviewee also seeks agreement from the interviewer with her *yeah*, ending in rising intonation. Her laughter (line 08) is a sign of the delicacy of the topic and/or of the action of resisting part of the interviewer's question. The interviewee's response thus deviates from the interviewer's agenda of showcasing the background of the interviewee for the audience.

As a result, the interviewer is put in the position of responding to the interviewee rather than proceeding with his line of questioning. Instead of aligning and responding to the request for confirmation, he next offers a characterization of the intent of his prior question: a positive assessment of the interviewee's *impressive background* (lines 09–11). The *oh* with which he begins his turn may signal a change of state (Heritage, 1984), a display of a "sudden" realization that the question could be heard as inappropriate. The interviewer's reformulation omits the problematic reference to a number of years.

Having dealt with the interviewee's "unexpected" response, the interviewer moves on quickly. He begins a new TCU with *but* (line 11) and proceeds to reference the report on the foundation's new framework in lines 12–15, which is to be the substance of the interview: *but what it- what it talks about here is*. He ultimately launches a request for the interviewee to explain the framework, partially shown (line 16).

Most immediately, *but*-prefacing enables the interviewer to, in a single turn, mark a shift from accounting for his prior question back to the main business of asking questions and moving the interview forward. However, it is worth noting that it is the interviewee's disaligning action of resisting the interviewer's question that prompts this refocusing work in the first place. *But* therefore serves to draw a line between diverging talk initiated by an "other" and talk that forwards the speaker's main agenda. Put another way, *but* marks the resumption of typical interviewer-interviewee roles and responsibilities: Interviewers ask questions, and interviewees respond.

Discussion and Conclusion

In the preceding analysis, we hope to have specified the interactional work that speakers engaged in communicating with the public can accomplish through the use of *but*-prefacing. Building on Schiffrin's (1987) work on *but* as a discourse marker that signals a speaker's return to a prior point, we find that *but*-prefacing marks the start of, or a return to, the expected course of action. It is most commonly used by speakers in our dataset following self-initiated divergences from the main business of a multi-unit turn: after they attend to ancillary matters, such as offering background or accomplishing other actions; attend to procedural matters, or issues relevant to managing the activity and maintaining progressivity; or attend to expectations regarding the content of the turn.

More rarely, *but*-prefacing is used to respond to other-initiated actions, a finding that may reflect a defining characteristic of the public interactions we have examined: participants' orientation to cooperation. Given that *but*-prefaced utterances can paint prior talk as off-topic, out-of-place, or otherwise "beside the main point," directing them to co-participants could be seen as a challenging move. Moreover, in spite of the constraints imposed by type of activity (moderated panel discussion) or format (webinar), participants in our dataset routinely perform aligning actions, for example, answer questions when asked. A concern for "doing collegiality" (Reddington, Clemente, Waring, & Yu, forthcoming) may in fact limit the need for refocusing work directed toward others.

In all cases, speakers leverage the contrastive power of *but* to draw a line between talk that is in some sense parenthetical to the main interactional agenda (e.g., conducting an interview or eliciting audience questions) and talk that moves it forward. While we have anecdotal evidence to suggest that a refocusing function of *but* is not unique to institutional talk, *but*-prefacing does appear to do special work in the activities that we have examined. Marking the boundary between parenthetical talk and the main point is one way in which speakers at public events, whether they are institutional representatives or audience members, display their accountability to the overhearing others for focusing on the business at hand: to ask a question when selected or respond when asked. In other words, through *but*-prefacing, speakers succinctly display awareness of a (self-initiated) digression and signal moving past it.

In addition to contributing to the growing body of conversation analytic work on discourse markers in naturally occurring interaction, we also hope to have offered a finding of direct relevance for the practitioner, the institutional representative who must engage in public interactions on a regular basis. The production of a single word in the midst of a lengthy turn can enable the speaker to quickly close down a digression and pivot to the main point, making it salient, and perhaps more comprehensible, for the recipient and the overhearing audience. Rather than viewing *but* as a superfluous addition to the beginning of an utterance, through a conversation analytic lens, we can appreciate it as a useful tool for solving the practical problem of "getting back to business."

Note

1 Preliminary analysis of Extracts 3, 6, and 11 appeared in Choe and Reddington (2018).

References

Bell, D. M. (1998). Cancellative discourse markers: A core/periphery approach. *Pragmatics. Quarterly Publication of the International Pragmatics Association (IPrA), 8*(4), 515–541.

Blakemore, D. (1989). Denial and contrast: A relevance theoretic analysis of *but*. *Linguistics and Philosophy, 12*(1), 15–37.

Blakemore, D. (2000). Indicators and procedures: *Nevertheless* and *but*. *Journal of Linguistics, 36*(3), 463–486.

Blakemore, D. (2002). *Relevance and linguistic meaning: The semantics and pragmatics of discourse*. New York: Cambridge University Press.

Bolden, G. (2006). Little words that matter: Discourse markers "so" and "oh" and the doing of other-attentiveness in social interaction. *Journal of Communication, 56*(4), 661–688.

Bolden, G. (2009). Implementing incipient actions: The discourse marker 'so' in English conversation. *Journal of Pragmatics, 41*, 974–998.

Carnie, A. (2013). *Syntax: A generative introduction* (3rd ed.). West Sussex, UK: Wiley-Blackwell.

Choe, A. T., & Reddington, E. (2018). *But*-prefacing for refocusing in public questioning and answering. *Studies in Applied Linguistics & TESOL, 18*(1), 44–50.

Crow, B. K. (1983). Topic shifts in couples' conversations. In R. T. Craig & K. Tracy (Eds.), *Conversational coherence* (pp. 137–156). Beverly Hills, CA: Sage.

Drake, V. (2015). Indexing uncertainty: The case of turn-final *or*. *Research on Language and Social Interaction, 48*(3), 301–318.

Fraser, B. (1996). Pragmatic markers. *Pragmatics, 6*(2), 167–190.

Fraser, B. (2008). *The discourse marker but in English*. Boston: Boston University.

Fraser, B. (2009). The English contrastive discourse marker *on the contrary*. In B. Fraser & K. Turner (Eds.), *Language in life, and a life in language: Jacob Mey—a festschrift* (pp. 87–95). Bingley: Emerald Group.

Fraser, B. (2013). Combinations of contrastive discourse markers in English. *International Review of Pragmatics, 5*, 318–340.

Goffman, E. (1981). *Forms of talk*. Philadelphia: University of Pennsylvania Press.

Halliday, M. A. K., & Hasan, R. (1976). *Cohesion in English*. London: Longman.

Heritage, J. (1984). A change-of-state token and aspects of its sequential placement. In J. M. Atkinson & J. Heritage (Eds.), *Structures of social action: Studies in conversation analysis* (pp. 299–345). Cambridge: Cambridge University Press.

Lakoff, R. (1971). *If*'s, *and*'s and *but*'s about conjunction. In C. J. Fillmore & D. T. Langendoen (Eds.), *Studies in linguistic semantics* (pp. 115–150). New York: Holt, Reinhart and Winston.

Park, I. (2010). Marking an impasse: The use of *anyway* as a sequence-closing device. *Journal of Pragmatics, 42*, 3283–3299.

Psathas, G. (1995). *Conversation analysis: The study of talk-in-interaction*. Thousand Oaks, CA: Sage.

Reddington, E., Clemente, I., Waring, H. Z., & Yu, D. (forthcoming). "Doing being collegial": Participants' positioning work in Q&A sessions. In C. Ilie (Ed.), *Questioning-answering practices across contexts and cultures*. Amsterdam: Benjamins.

Schegloff, E. A. (1980). Preliminaries to preliminaries: "Can I ask you a question?" *Sociological Inquiry, 50*(3–4), 104–152.

Schegloff, E. A., & Lerner, G. H. (2009). Beginning to respond: *Well*-prefaced responses to *wh-* questions. *Research on Language and Social Interaction, 42*(2), 91–115.

Schegloff, E. A., & Sacks, H. (1973). Opening up closings. *Semiotica, 7*, 289–327.

Schiffrin, D. (1987). *Discourse markers*. New York: Cambridge University Press.

Waring, H. Z. (2003). "Also" as a discourse marker: Its use in disjunctive and disaffiliative environments. *Discourse Studies, 5*, 415–436.

Waring, H. Z. (2012). Doing disaffiliation with *now*-prefaced utterances. *Language and Communication, 32*, 265–275.

6

Curating the Q&A: The Art of Moderating Webinars

Allie Hope King
Teachers College, Columbia University

Introduction

In recent years, webinars have become a common, if not a standard, approach for individuals and institutions to disseminate information to a wide audience that is able to participate remotely. Short for *web-based seminar*, webinars can cover an indefinite number of topics and can be organized in a variety of manners. Many include a "question and answer" (Q&A) segment during which audience members can petition hosts to clarify, expand upon, or otherwise assist with questions that remain. As would be the case in any information-dissemination event, it is presumably important to all parties involved that these questions are handled in a satisfactory manner and that the responses given by the webinar hosts are understandable for the audience. With this in mind, the million-dollar question for anyone putting the time and resources into giving a webinar is: What *precisely* can hosts do when interacting with their audience to ensure an effective, informative, and engaging Q&A experience?

In a typical webinar, the hosts are usually employees or guest affiliates of the organization holding the event, and one of these hosts acts as the moderator, whose role is to facilitate the event, including the Q&A interaction. In some ways, the responsibilities of this individual are tied to the technological setup of the event. For example, many webinars enable participants to see and speak to each other directly through video conferencing and, during the Q&A,

the platform might allow for actions such as "raising hands" for audience members to signal their wish to take the floor and ask a question. In this context, a moderator's role may simply involve calling on the individuals, who then present their own question in the interaction. However, many webinars are *voice-only*, meaning that while hosts may use slides as a visual aid to accompany their talk, there are no video conferencing features, and audience members are limited to using a text-chat feature to interact with the hosts during the Q&A. Within this particular dynamic, the moderator can take on a complex "third-party" role: On the one hand, they must act as a proxy for the audience members, "voicing" written questions aloud for all to hear, and effectively serving as an interactional bridge between the webinar attendees and the other hosts; on the other hand, the moderator is also responsible for ensuring that the overall interaction runs smoothly and efficiently, and that questions are addressed in a timely and comprehensible manner.

In fields such as distance education, and science and technology, there has been a fair amount of interdisciplinary work on conducting webinars, which falls under the umbrella of "best practices" literature. While the recommendations might differ slightly according to the context, subject matter, or target audience, the myriad books, online articles, and even webinars that offer information on how to effectively run a webinar share similar suggestions. Unsurprisingly, many authors (e.g., Argon, 2012; Carvalho-Silva, Garcia, Morgan, Brooksbank & Dunham, 2018) emphasize the importance of choosing software and technology that is both reliable and easy for hosts and audience members to navigate. Bedford's (2016) summary of existing "best practices" materials available online indicates that many of the popular suggestions for webinar hosting center around pre-event planning. Whether the authors propose doing a practice run, surveying audience members in advance to better prepare content, or choosing a particular day of the week to host the event, the general consensus seems to be that producing a successful webinar is highly dependent on the type and amount of work that takes place *before* the actual event.

Most of the available work on webinars is non-empirical and is based on the authors' personal experiences organizing and participating in these online events. However, some of the literature on webinar design or execution does involve empirical research, and this work tends to touch upon how to moderate and involve the audience. For example, Lande (2011) systematically reviewed the existing "how-to" literature. One important finding was that empirical studies on webinar effectiveness were rare among the resources available. As a result, Lande's report focused predominantly on "white papers" and other online informational articles. Among the themes that she identified, Lande found one recurrent suggestion to be that, since moderators have to manage multiple components of the event, including the technology, the presentation of audience questions, and the responsibility to ensure that the overall Q&A interaction runs smoothly, it is important that webinar hosts avoid taking on the role of *both* a moderator and a presenter. Zoumenou et al. (2015) conducted an empirical study that combined the results of a literature review and interview data to identify "best practices" as well. One of several assertions that they made was that it is important to allow participants to interact with the hosts by utilizing certain technological features to enable them to ask questions. In fact, the authors claimed that the key to an effective webinar is interactivity because providing participants with the opportunity to communicate directly with each other during a synchronous (i.e., real-time) event can foster a sense of connectedness, community, and engagement. However, beyond mentioning some of the special interactive features available on different software platforms that can purportedly enhance the webinar, this work does not specify how or when to implement these features during the interaction, nor do the authors paint a concrete picture of how, *exactly*, interactivity correlates with a webinar's effectiveness.

In general, literature on conducting webinars uses hosts' accumulated experience as a resource to provide "tips" that could possibly lead to smoother, more effective, and more engaging webinars. Yet, while these suggestions may be broadly useful, more in-depth analysis of actual webinar interaction has the potential to not only offer empirical support for their validity, but also provide much-needed specification to enable efficient execution of these "best practices." The purpose of this study is to offer such specificity by examining naturally occurring interaction from several synchronous webinar Q&As with a focus on how the moderators facilitate both the typed-in questions from audience members and the spoken participation of other hosts.

Data

The data were seventeen webinars from a larger collection of recorded online events hosted by the Better Living Health Foundation (BLHF), a major philanthropic organization in the United States. Each of the synchronous webinars was recorded by the foundation and then made available online to eventually reach a wider, non-present audience. In general, all of the webinars aimed to communicate with external audiences about the organization's mission and programs devoted to improving public health; however, there were a variety of more specific objectives among them. For example, several webinars focused on the process of completing a grant application with the organization, while others were more theme-based and involved host panelists discussing and answering questions about particular health-related projects or experiences. The webinars selected for the present analysis reflected the most commonly used format in that they included slide-based presentations and Q&As which relied solely on a text-chat option for audience members to ask questions. Each webinar had one moderator and between two and six other foundation representatives, who included foundation officers as well as individuals from other organizations affiliated in some manner with the foundation. In addition, there was an unknown number[1] of audience member participants attending each event online. Because the underlying interest of the study was in the moderator's role during Q&A interaction, the analysis focused on moderator talk in question-answer sequences. Each question-answer sequence from the seventeen Q&A sessions was transcribed and analyzed according to the principles of conversation analysis (CA). This led to the discovery of a set of moderator practices that were prevalent across the data.

Analysis and Findings

As noted earlier, in order for audience members in this context to "communicate" with foundation representatives during the Q&A, they had to type in their questions via the online platform; the moderator then selected and presented questions aloud for all to hear. Extract 1 provides an example.

(1) first question
```
01   MO:         H. the first question we have Nikki is for
02               you. .HHH and it's (.) ((reading voice))-↑who
03               will review <my: proposal.>
04               (1.8)
05   NIK:        sure. >thanks Emma,< ↑actually ah it gets
06               a lot of ↑eye:s,
```

Moderators in these Q&A sessions were found to consistently deploy a handful of practices to manage both the delivery of and the response to audience questions. The following analysis[2] will begin by describing moderator practices associated with presenting the audience member's question in the first turn of question-answer sequences. This will be followed by a description of one practice that moderators use to manage the participation of other hosts, who respond to the questions in the second turn. At each stage of the analysis, the aim will be to show precisely how these practices allow moderators to shape key components of question-answer sequences in ways that not only facilitate the efficiency and progressivity of the interaction, but also increase the potential for understanding and even engagement during the Q&A session.

Presenting the Question

Analysis of the first turn of question-answer sequences revealed that moderators use a number of interactional resources when delivering questions on behalf of the audience members. This section will describe two practices that were prevalent in the data: *question preliminaries* and *question animation*. As will be shown, moderators use these devices to organize and present the typed-in questions in a systematic way.

Question Preliminaries

With notable regularity throughout data, moderators were found to do *question preliminaries,* or to produce talk in the questioning turn prior to delivering the audience question itself. These preliminaries were typically done to group similar questions, announce question topics, and identify question authors.

Extract 2 takes place at the beginning of the Q&A session from a webinar about the application process for a particular grant. The presentation has just come to a close, and the moderator announces the start of the Q&A and launches into the first question.

(2) grouping
```
    01    MO:   →      so the first question that we've received
    02          →      several times is if the s̲lides and r̲ecording of
    03                 this presentation will be available online
    04                 °following the call.°
```

Following a *so*-prefaced turn-beginning that precedes the sequence-initiating action (Bolden, 2009), the moderator produces a question preliminary, announcing in lines 01–02 that the impending question is one that has been submitted *several times* by audience members. Unlike most of the examples that will be described in the analysis to come, the moderator does not seem to be using a *reading voice* and reading this question word-for-word. One indication of this is that, rather than producing the complete question as it might have been typed by the questioner, the moderator produces an embedded question that is syntactically cohesive with her own immediately preceding talk in line 02, making the turn appear more like a paraphrased version of what was likely submitted in writing. The turn also lacks paralinguistic features such as exaggerated pitch variation, which moderators were found to deploy to signal a shift into voicing an audience member's question verbatim (see the next section on *question animation*). Instead, the moderator appears to have grouped a collection of similar items from within the written set of questions. By explicating that the question was submitted *several* times, this particular preliminary highlights the commonality and, therefore, relevance of the question.

While preliminaries that do grouping may increase efficiency and highlight relevance, it was more common in the data for moderators to produce preliminaries that supplement the question with other types of information. The next example shows the moderator announcing the topic of the question prior to reading it. Extract 3 takes place shortly after Extract 2 above.

(3) topicalizing
```
01    MO:   →    u::h so a budgeti:ng question?
02                 ((reading voice))-will we need to travel to: BLHF
03                 uh award announcement, or pay for
04                 our awardees to travel (.) there,
```

Following a lengthened hesitation marker *uh* in line 01, the moderator again uses a *so*-prefaced turn-beginning to initiate a new sequence. She then produces a question preliminary consisting only of the noun phrase *a budgeting question* before launching into reading the question about responsibility for travel expenses in line 02. By pre-labeling the impending question with its topic or subject matter, in this case by announcing that what is about to come is a "budgeting question," the moderator can catch the attention of other audience members who may have similar questions and alert those panelists who are responsible for answering finance-related inquiries.

Whereas question preliminaries that do grouping or announce the topic give key information about the question *content*, in the next example, the preliminary offers information about the question's *author*. Extract 4 comes from a webinar on one of the foundation's large-scale health-related projects and takes place a few minutes into the Q&A.

(4) identifying
```
01    MO:   →    .hh (.) thanks for that.=we have a
02           →    ↑question from Kaylee:.
03                 ((reading voice))-are chi:ld data available.
04                 or is it just adults.
```

Line 01 begins as the moderator is closing one question-answer sequence with *thanks for that* and immediately launching a new question which she attributes to a specific audience member, *Kaylee*. After identifying its author, the moderator delivers the question. Here, the preliminary provides an overt signal to one person in particular, Kaylee, that she should listen closely to the upcoming talk. Arguably, it also adds a personal touch to the job of being a proxy for an otherwise nameless set of audience attendees.

The examples of question preliminaries above represent the common iterations of what was found to be a prevalent practice in the dataset. While each preliminary provides a distinct type of information about the question it precedes, an important underlying feature of all three is the property of "pre-ness." Schegloff (2007) described "pre-ness" as a free-floating property that "has relevance to and bearing on some action or utterance projected to occur" (p. 44). The question preliminary is such a device that enables moderators to provide key information about what listeners are about to hear before they hear it, which may facilitate their ability to follow what comes.

Question Animation

In the voice-only webinar context, moderators recurrently use specific paralinguistic features when presenting or *animating* the typed-in questions on behalf of audience members. Prior interactional research (e.g., Goffman, 1981; Levinson, 1988) has shown that speakers may signal different roles during the production of their talk through the deployment of certain prosodic cues. In particular, speakers utilize paralinguistic features like volume, prosody, or pausing as instruments in order to, for example, differentiate the distinct voices in reported talk from other discourse in a turn (Couper-Kuhlen, 1998; Günthner, 1999). Unlike reported speech, in which the speaker is typically recollecting and often paraphrasing talk that occurred at an earlier time, in the webinar context, the moderator has the text visible in front of her as a different kind of resource to draw upon while delivering reported *text*.

While moderators use a number of paralinguistic features simultaneously, of interest here is the use of pre-question pausing and big inbreaths as well as exaggerated pitch variations during question delivery. These paralinguistic features combine to do special work when moderators ask questions on behalf of audience members.

Extract 5 comes from another webinar on grant applications. Throughout her turn, the moderator employs a number of question animation features in the presentation of one question.

(5) question animation
```
    01   MO:   →      the first question: .hh i:s (0.2)
    02         →      ((reading voice))-↑you ↑indicated this program
    03                spe↑cifically targets funding ↓#research.#=
```

```
04                  yes:,=we $did indicate that many ↓#times$#.
05        →         .HHH ((reading voice))-a:nd (.) >program or policy<
06                  implementation is ↑not eligi↓ble. (.)
07                  so is <evalu↑atio:n> of the implementation of
08                  <a program or policy (.) considered re↓search.> (.)
09                  .H ↑Nikki do you wanna elaborate on that a bit,
```

After initiating the sequence with the preliminary *the first question is* in line 01, the moderator pauses for 0.2 seconds before beginning to deliver the question. While pauses, or intra-turn silences within the speech of one speaker (Sacks, Schegloff & Jefferson, 1974), have been linked to such phenomena as trouble associated with a word search (see, e.g., Goodwin & Goodwin, 1986) or the think time that a speaker needs to come up with subsequent talk (see, e.g., McHoul, 1978), the frequency of pause placement just prior to the audience question in these data suggests that the silence might be more of a gearing-up action associated with the upcoming question delivery. In this sense, the pre-reading pause is more akin to non-rhythmic pauses found immediately prior to reported speech (see, e.g., Couper-Kuhlen, 1998; Klewitz & Couper-Kuhlen, 1999), where it delimits a boundary between the different voices in play.

In line 02, the moderator starts to deliver the question, which begins with a summary of some prior representative comments on what the grant would fund. As she launches into the question content, the moderator raises her pitch on the first two words of the question *you* and *indicated*. This pitch alteration functions to create a distinction between the "moderator voice" found in line 01 and the "animator voice" (Goffman, 1981) that delivers the reported text beginning in line 02. As the moderator reaches the end of the first part of the audience question in line 03, she lowers her pitch to such an extent that she produces the last word *research* with a vocal fry. She then suspends her delivery of the question to address the audience member's summation and confirm the understanding that the grant offered is indeed limited to funding research (line 04). Similar to the pitch raise found at the question's beginning, here pitch lowering at the end of a segment of reported text creates a marked contrast between voices as the moderator shifts from delivery *of* the question into response *to* the question, a move that is also evidenced by the pronoun switch from *you* in line 02 to *we* in line 04.

After affirming the accuracy of the audience member's recap of presentation details, in line 05, the moderator produces a notable inbreath just before she returns to the task of delivering the audience question. While big inbreaths are often an indication that a speaker is about to launch into a multi-unit turn (MUT) (Wong & Waring, 2010), this inbreath comes in the middle of an MUT and appears to be less of a signal of the duration of upcoming talk and more of an audible cue that the moderator is moving out of the moderator voice and back into the animator voice. She then proceeds through the remainder of the question in lines 05–08, and her pitch on the final word of the question, *research,* is once again lowered beyond the typical falling intonation found at the end of a turn-constructional unit (TCU). Similar to the pitch pattern found at the end of line 03, the falling pitch that marks the end of the question and the reported text makes the animator talk hearably distinct from the immediately subsequent moderator talk in line 09, where the moderator calls on representative Nikki to handle the question.

The paralinguistic features described above—pre-question pausing and inbreaths, as well as pitch raising and lowering at points in moderator talk such as the beginnings and endings of reported text—all function similarly and simultaneously to establish an audible boundary in the questioning turn between the moderator talk that is organizing the interaction and the animator talk that is doing reported text of audience member questions. Overall, these question animation features, in tandem with other paralinguistic practices such as reduced speed or exaggerated word stress, provide concrete and hearable cues that may facilitate the overall listening experience during the Q&A. On the one hand, the frequently occurring pre-reading pauses and inbreaths signal that the moderator is gearing up to voice a question, which may be an attention-getting device. On the other hand, the exaggerated raising and lowering of pitch at question beginnings and endings may further signpost the moderator's progress through the question delivery by creating an audible boundary around the question itself through the establishing of and distinguishing between two voices. It can be argued that a moderator's implementation of question animation is potentially consequential for the hearing of and understandability of the questions in the voice-only webinar Q&A context.

Managing the Response

The role of the moderator in this dataset was found to go beyond delivering the questions to also managing the responses. This was done primarily through the use of *respondent selection*. The principal component of respondent selection involves the moderator's use of a personal or institution name (e.g., *the first question will be for BLHF*) in the questioning turn of the sequence to designate who should handle the response. This section will first illustrate how respondent selection is done. It will then be shown how the absence of this practice can lead to significant interactional trouble.

Extract 6 is a continuation of Extract 5 above. Here, the focus will be on what comes after the question delivery, when the moderator turns the floor over for another foundation representative to respond.

(6) post-question position
```
01    MO:           .HHH ((reading voice))-a:nd (.) >program or policy<
02                  implementation is ↑not eligi↓ble. (.)
03                  so is <evalu↑atio:n of the implementation of
04                  <a program or policy (.) considered re↓search.> (.)
05          →       .H ↑Nikki do you wanna elaborate on that a bit,
06                  (0.5)
07    NI:   →       sure. u::m (.) .tch the ↑answer is the evaluation
08                  of a- a- program or policy (.) ca:n be research,
```

The moderator finishes reading the question in line 04, and then in line 05, she selects foundation representative Nikki by name to respond, followed by the invitation *do you wanna elaborate on that a bit*. After a 0.5-second gap, which could be related to the participants not being in the same room or the need for her microphone to be unmuted, Nikki produces an agreement token *sure* (line 07), acknowledging that she will answer the question. She then launches into her response.

Extract 6 provides a straightforward example of respondent selection, and it represents what was prevalent throughout the data. In this instance, there is a smooth progression through the sequence—the moderator animates the audience question, and then verbally selects a respondent, who quickly offers a response. Here, the selection is done after the question is read, in a *post-question position*; however, it can also be done in a *pre-question position*, or before the question has been read, as Extract 7 will demonstrate.

This instance comes from another webinar on the grant proposal submission process involving the same foundation representatives. As the extract begins, the moderator is moving into a new question-answer sequence.

(7) pre-question position
```
01    MO:   →      .tch so the ↑next question hh. u:h let's
02          →      ↑turn back to you Nikki for this one, -t's
03                 a great question, (.)
04                 .H ((reading voice))-↑have ↑you considered referring
05                 projects to: program officers for other
06                 funding opportunities within the #foundation.#
07                 (0.2)
08    NI:   →      .hh u:h y- absolutely.=u:m >actually< our
09                 colleagues in the foundation ↑f:requently
```

Similar to Extract 5, the moderator begins with a preliminary *the next question* (line 01), seemingly about to begin reading the next question. However, instead of launching into the question, she pauses to insert a personal name. This mid-TCU deployment of the respondent selection practice pre-selects Nikki to handle the impending question. After characterizing the upcoming question as a *great* one and pausing briefly, the moderator finally begins to read in line 04, arriving at the end of the question in line 06. Following a brief gap, in line 08, representative Nikki takes her turn, moving smoothly into an affirmative response.

As these examples demonstrate, respondent selection is done by naming an individual or, less commonly, the institution that the individual represents. As shown above, respondent selection can occur in either a pre- or a post-question position, with the pre-question position occurring more commonly in this dataset. Again, it is relevant to bring up the notion of "pre-ness" (Schegloff, 2007) to consider how respondent selection may shape the interaction. When the moderator fronts a foundation representative's name prior to reading the question, that individual receives an overt signal that they are responsible for providing an answer to the question that is about to be shared. This ostensibly allows the individual an opportunity to pay closer attention to the impending talk. In addition to preparing the next speaker, such selection may also provide some clarity on a more global level for the audience. In particular, the moderator's use of representatives' personal names or the name of their institution could reflect one way of explicating which *individual* at the institution, or which *institution* within the group of organizations attending, is responsible for the information connected with the question. This would be useful in this context given that audience members may wish to contact foundation representatives after the webinar with follow-up questions.

The final instance demonstrates what might happen when respondent selection is *not* done. Extract 8 is from a webinar in which foundation representatives Cody and Kristoff have been invited to share their experiences with the audience. The extract begins as the moderator is closing one question-answer sequence and moving on to the next question.

(8) no selection

```
01    MO:           .H thanks Cody, thanks Cody.=so:- (0.2) .HH
02                  so I lied earlier thi- ↑this now will be our
03                  last $question?$ .HH u::m uh <and it's
04                  a really interesting one which is
05                  ((reading voice))-↑how do you: navigate issues
06                  of (0.2) intellectual <#property.#> (.)
07                  so either in terms of formal structures
08                  <related> to ownership of developed ↑outputs,
09                  (0.2)
10    MO:           or more informal concerns of the
11                  appropriate attribu:tion of #innovations.# (.)
12                  um I think a- a really interesting topic.
13           →      =a:nd who- (.) whoever would like to start.
14                  (1.8)
15    CO:   →       [.hh yeah. we: can certainly (.) °uh-° ]
16    KR:   →       [.hh I can provide ou:r general prov- ]
17                  (0.2)
18    CO:   →       go [ahead.=Kristoff. ]
19    KR:   →          [go ahead.=Cody?]
20                  (0.5)
21    KR:   →       [(syl syl)]
22    CO:   →       [I'll just ] say we certainly dealt with this as this
23                  is part of ou:::r uh co-laboratory as I called it.=
```

In line 01, the moderator closes the prior sequence with her repeated *thanks* and representative Cody's name, and then humorously claims to have lied, stating that the forthcoming question will in fact be the last one, and not the one she had given that status to earlier in the interaction (lines 02–03). She characterizes the impending question as an *interesting* one (line 04) and then reads the question aloud (lines 05–11). After reading and again noting that the topic is interesting, in line 13, the moderator opens the floor for a response, directing the invitation to speak to *whoever would like to start*. Following a notable gap of 1.8 seconds, in lines 15 and 16, both Cody and Kristoff begin to speak at precisely the same time, and then they both cut themselves off after a long overlap. Following a short gap (line 17), they both begin to speak again at the same time. This time, they each try to resolve their inadvertent competition for the floor by selecting the other by name (lines 18 and 19). After another gap, and yet another short overlap (lines 21 and 22), Kristoff relinquishes the floor, and Cody goes on to give his response.

Widening the lens to consider all three extracts in this section together, a few more points can be made about some of the local effects of respondent selection. Perhaps most significantly, this practice seems to be a resource for moderators to signpost the interaction in a way that partially dictates how the second turn of the question-answer sequence will go. Whereas the sequences in Extracts 6 and 7 unfold without a hitch, a substantial amount of trouble occurs in Extract 8 when the moderator does not use an explicit address term to select a specific representative to handle the question. Interestingly, we also see in Extract 8 that the two representatives resort to using each other's names to try to exit their jumble of overlap. Thus, it could be argued that respondent selection is not only facilitative for the progressivity of the transition from the first- to the second-pair part of the sequence, but a moderator's failure to use the practice could be so problematic that the participants are forced to deploy the practice themselves to move the sequence forward.

Discussion and Conclusion

The analysis has shown that, in the institutional context of voice-only webinars, moderators regularly adopt the role of a "third-party" participant and use particular practices to construct or facilitate components of the question-answer sequence on behalf of the two other groups of participants: the audience, who are limited to chatting in their questions to the hosts, and the other foundation representatives, who must respond to the audience questions clearly and effectively. In particular, the moderator utilizes question preliminaries to organize and signpost questions in a number of ways, which include grouping similar inquiries into one sequence as well as announcing the topic or the identity of the question's author. Whereas grouping might increase the efficiency of the Q&A session, identifying the topic and author of the question can provide important forward-pointing information for listeners about what is to come. Question animation, on the other hand, can facilitate the listening itself. The moderator's simultaneous use of paralinguistic features such as pre-question pausing and inbreaths, along with exaggerated pitch variation at question beginnings and endings, establishes an audible boundary around the question itself. This boundary marking can highlight the question content and aid comprehension. At the same time, it allows the moderator to embody the task of *doing being the voice of the audience* and speaking as their proxy in the Q&A interaction in ways that more closely resemble a dyadic exchange and enliven what could otherwise unfold as a monotonous chain of question-answer sequences. As such, question animation might serve to make the listening experience more engaging or, at the very least, dialogic.

In addition to introducing the audience questions, moderators also use respondent selection as they stage the responses to those questions. This occurs in either a pre- or a post-question position, with the former being more common. Similar to question preliminaries, the "pre-ness" of respondent selection also provides listeners with an explicit sign of what is to come, specifically *who* will be responsible for handling the upcoming question, thus promoting the progressivity of the sequence and, therefore, the clarity and quality of the interaction in general. It also provides pertinent information for audience members, specifically the names of foundation representatives or institutions that may be resources for follow-up. Although the data do not offer any clear evidence, it is possible that the pre-question position is more helpful to the selected representatives who may then pay closer attention to the question as it is being read. In short, the greater degree of "pre-ness" might enable moderators to better prepare their colleagues for impending talk and action. Separately, but relatedly, when moderators produce invitation talk directed at the designated respondent, such as that in Extract 6 (*do you wanna elaborate on that a bit*) before turning over the floor, they might also be affording the respondent slightly more time to prepare to answer the question, which may be important if the question is a complex one.

The frequency of respondent selection in these data is also interesting in light of prior research on speaker selection in interaction. In an analysis of next speaker selection in everyday multiparty interaction, Lerner (2003) pointed out that "if one wants to direct a sequence-initiating action *unambiguously* [emphasis added] to a particular co-participant, then one can address that participant with a personal name or other address term" (p. 184). While names and other explicit address terms in Lerner's data were "arguably the strongest forms of address available," they were not the most prevalent. In fact, he stated that they seemed to be "used primarily under specific circumstances in which they are deployed to do more than simply specify whom the speaker is addressing" (p. 184). The present analysis suggests that the use of address terms for next speaker selection may be more common in a voice-only, institutional, multiparty context like a webinar Q&A where the participants may have no visual access to cues about who might take a turn.[3] In Lerner's study, gaze was quite commonly employed as a way of explicitly selecting a next speaker. In voice-only webinars, by contrast, gaze is not an available resource for turn-taking. Instead, an explicit address term can serve as an audible signpost for the moderator to unambiguously allocate the next turn.

Considering the systematic implementation of the multitude of practices described above, we can appreciate how moderating Q&A sessions in voice-only webinars is not a simple endeavor. Instead, it involves a great deal of forethought and decision-making on a moment-to-moment basis about both the organization and the presentation of the material at hand. In many ways, the art of effectively moderating a voice-only webinar is akin to the task of curating a collection for an exhibit. A term often associated with the visual arts, curation entails the assembling, arranging, and presentation of some type of collection with an end goal of bringing an engaging and specific experience to life for an audience. Webinar moderators are charged in their "third-party" position with the job of curating a well-organized, informative, and engaging Q&A experience for all participants involved in the event, a task they achieve in part by implementing the practices discussed here such as assembling similar inquiries, framing and spotlighting questions, and sign-posting their talk to enhance participants' listening experience (see also Yu and Tadic, this volume).

Given the myriad ways in which moderators work to curate the Q&A experience for the other participants, it makes sense that webinar hosts are discouraged from trying to fill both a moderator and a panelist role in the same webinar (e.g., Lande, 2011). In addition, this analysis crystalizes some of the other recommendations found in the "best practices" literature with respect to the importance of pre-planning and fostering engagement. Specifically, we may suggest the following for moderating voice-only webinars:

1. Decide how questions will be delivered and representatives called upon *before* the event, and share this information with all hosts. For high-stakes webinars, doing a practice run-through with sample questions can help all hosts know what to expect.
2. Review the set of submitted questions and group similar questions to paraphrase into one question—repeating the same question can waste time.
3. Announce the question topic before reading the question to alert listeners to questions that might pertain to them.
4. If available, state the name of the question's author when reading the question. This will alert the author before their question is answered, and it can also create a more personalized feel.
5. Read questions aloud in a lively and animated voice (i.e., use pausing, louder volume, pitch variation, and stress on key words) to help listeners hear each question clearly and to keep them engaged.
6. Choose the best respondent based on the nature of the question and then name that person or institution, preferably prior to reading the question. This will help prepare representatives and will prevent multiple people from speaking at once. It will also remind listeners of which people or institutions are associated with what information.

These "tips" constitute some empirically grounded best practices. Further CA research is needed to uncover additional practices behind the art of moderating webinars.

Notes

1   The dataset did not include information such as the number of audience members attending any given webinar.
2   Preliminary analysis of Extracts 6, 7, and 8 appeared in King (2018).
3   Details about whether foundation representatives were in the same room during the webinar recordings were also unavailable in the dataset. However, there is evidence in the data that at least some representatives joined remotely.

References

Argon, M. (2012, May). *The five things you must know about webinar audio*. Retrieved from http://www.webattract.com/docs/ebook/TheFiveThingsYouMustKnowAboutWebinarAudio_eBook_august2012.pdf.

Bedford, N. (2016). Webinar best practices: A summary of existing recommendations. Retrieved from Carleton University website http://carleton.ca/communityfirst/. DOI: http://dx.doi.org/10.22215/cfice-2016-06.

Bolden, G. (2009). Implementing incipient actions: The discourse marker "so" in English conversation. *Journal of Pragmatics, 41*(5), 974–998.

Carvalho-Silva, D., Garcia, L., Morgan, S. L., Brooksbank, C., & Dunham, I. (2018, November). *Ten simple rules for delivering live distance training in bioinformatics across the globe using webinars*. PLOS Computational Biology, *14*(11). Retrieved from https://doi.org/10.1371/journal.pcbi.1006419.

Couper-Kuhlen, E. (1998). Coherent voicing: On prosody in conversational reported speech. *InLiSt. Interaction and Linguistic Structures, 1*, 1–28.

Goffman, E. (1981). *Forms of talk*. Oxford: Blackwell.

Goodwin, M. H., & Goodwin, C. (1986). Gesture and coparticipation in the activity of searching for a word. *Semiotica, 62*(1/2), 51–75.

Günthner, S. (1999). Polyphony and the 'layering of voices' in reported dialogues: An analysis of the use of prosodic devices in everyday reported speech. *Journal of Pragmatics, 31*(5), 685–708.

King, A. H. (2018). Doing being the moderator: Use of "respondent selection" during webinar Q&As. *Studies in Applied Linguistics & TESOL, 18*(1), 23–30.

Klewitz, G., & Couper-Kuhlen, E. (1999). Quote–unquote? The role of prosody in the contextualization of reported speech sequences. *Pragmatics, 9*(4), 459–485.

Lande, L. M. (2011). *Webinar best practices: From invitation to evaluation*. Unpublished doctoral dissertation. University of Wisconsin-Stout, Wisconsin.

Lerner, G. H. (2003). Selecting next speaker: The context-sensitive operation of a context-free organization. *Language in Society, 32*(2), 177–201.

Levinson, S. C. (1988). Putting linguistics on a proper footing: Explorations in Goffman's participation framework. In P. Drew & A. Wootton (Eds.), *Erving Goffman: Exploring the interaction order* (pp. 161–227). Oxford: Polity Press.

McHoul, A. (1978). The organization of turns at formal talk in the classroom. *Language in Society, 7*(2), 183–213.

Sacks, H., Schegloff, E., & Jefferson, G. (1974). A simplest systematics for the organization of turn-taking for conversation. *Language, 50,* 696–735.

Schegloff, E. A. (2007). *Sequence organization in interaction: A primer in conversation analysis* (Vol. 1). Cambridge: Cambridge University Press.

Wong, J., & Waring, H. Z. (2010). *Conversation analysis and second language pedagogy: A guide for ESL/EFL teachers.* New York: Routledge.

Zoumenou, V., Sigman-Grant, M., Coleman, G., Malekian, F., Zee, J. M., Fountain, B. J., & Marsh, A. (2015). Identifying best practices for an interactive webinar. *Journal of Family & Consumer Sciences, 107*(2), 62–69.

7

Narrating the Visual in Webinar Q&As

Di Yu and Nadja Tadic
Teachers College, Columbia University

Introduction

Visual phenomena, including the use of gaze to attend to bodily-visual conduct and other semiotic resources in interaction, have long been a topic of interest in ethnomethodology and conversation analysis (EMCA) research (Goodwin, 2000; Nishizaka, 2000). The role of visual conduct as an interactional resource is particularly salient in technology-mediated contexts, where the "delicacy" of recognizing and coordinating gaze and gestures is often distorted or lost (Heath & Luff, 1993). Particularly in webinars during which a webcam is not used, participants not only lack visual access to each other but are also, given their different participation roles (e.g., presenter, audience member), privileged with different levels of visual access to how the activities in the webinar are displayed on their computer screens. In this chapter, we examine how such asymmetrical visual access is consequential for organizing webinar talk and how webinar moderators use what is visibly available on their computer screens or in their physical environment to remediate the visual asymmetry among participants in order to better manage question-answer segments (Q&As) in webinars.

In face-to-face interaction, participants orient to each other's gaze and bodily-visual conduct in the process of meaning making (Goodwin, 2000), whether it is to do speaker transition, time a turn entrance, or perform other actions, which suggests that visual conduct, together with a host of other semiotic resources, is essential in the production of social actions. It is not, in other words, a discrete, isolated, physiological phenomenon, but is embedded in the larger process of social action as an orderly, visible, and socially organized phenomenon (Nishizaka, 2000). Given this dependency on visual perception as a crucial resource for managing social interaction, it would be particularly interesting to explore participants' conduct in visually asymmetrical or restrictive settings.

Indeed, prior research on technology- or computer-mediated interaction has remarked on the potential challenges made relevant by the unique interactional features of such environments, such as turn-taking in chat-based interactions (Garcia & Jacobs, 1999) as well as participants' partially shared physical contexts and quasi-co-presence (Tudini & Liddicoat, 2017). Even for visually mediated environments with the use of a webcam, participants do not engage in mutual gaze as they would in in-person interactions, which renders the coordination of gaze and gesture difficult (Heath & Luff, 1993; Tudini & Liddicoat, 2017). Given the potential challenges faced by participants when navigating environments where visual resources are lacking, investigating the practices employed to remediate such "fractured ecologies" would be illuminating (Luff et al., 2003).

Data

Data consist of six publicly available audio recordings of webinars organized by the Better Living Health Foundation, a philanthropic foundation in the United States. These webinars are designed either to explicate specific grant opportunities to prospective applicants or to organize experts and practitioners in the field for discussions. Participants include foundation representatives, program officers, representatives from foundation-affiliated institutions, and prospective applicants interested in receiving grants from the foundation. During the webinars, the participants have the option to type in questions via a chat box in the web-conferencing platform (see anonymized screenshot of the webinar platform in Figure 7.1), virtually raise their hands (see Figure 7.2), and/or call in with questions or comments after being nominated by the moderator. A few features of this interactional context may be noted. First, although foundation representatives might share a physical space with each other, they are not in a shared physical space with external audience members. Representatives, consequently, must rely exclusively on audial resources

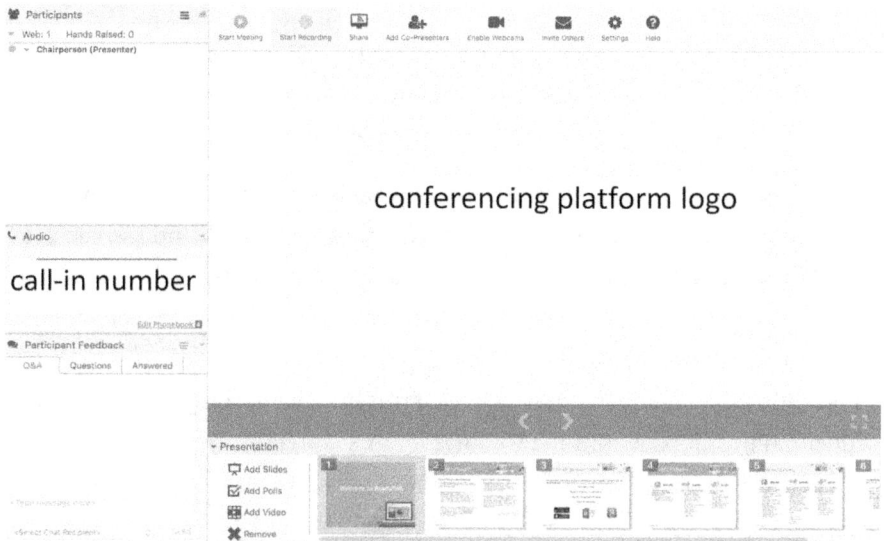

Figure 7.1 Webinar interface.

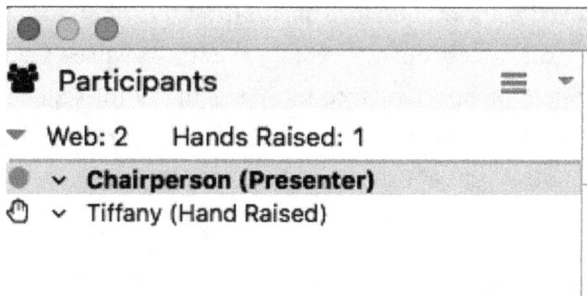

Figure 7.2 Participant raises hand virtually.

(i.e., voices and system sounds) and limited visual resources (e.g., chat box, participant list, presentation slides). Second, foundation representatives typically serve as moderators and thus have greater interactional privileges such as moving the presentation slides, muting and unmuting other participants, and seeing the entire list of participants as well as the "raised hands."

Based on audio-recordings of six webinars, we located seventeen instances where foundation representatives describe what is visually accessible to them on their screen to account for and project different types of further actions during webinars. A prototypical case of the phenomenon is shown in the following extract:

(1) Jane Smith
```
01    MO:         u:m:, okay I see that Jane Smith has her
02                hand raised.= Jane go ahead and hit
03                star seven on your phone?
```

As can be seen, the moderator introduces what is visually available to her with *I see that* (line 01), moves to select the next speaker (line 02), and instructs her to call into the webinar with her phone (lines 02–03). We term this practice of describing what is visually accessible "narrating the visual." It typically follows the formulation of *I + (don't) see/be looking at + description of visual perception*. In the following section, we describe what this practice accomplishes in various sequential positions within the webinar Q&A segments.

Analysis and Findings

In this section, we present the analysis of six excerpts[1] in which "narrating the visual" is deployed as the moderator's means to address the issue of participants' asymmetrical visual access during webinar events. As will be seen, the practice may: (1) provide a prospective account, particularly for sequence closing or initiation; (2) provide a retrospective account, particularly for a delayed action; or (3) provide both a retrospective and a prospective account.

Providing a Prospective Account

Our first excerpt features an instance of a moderator (MO) transitioning from an interactive Q&A component of the webinar (having muted webinar participants, as indicated by the automated voice [AT] in the transcript) to another component of the webinar—a presentation on the foundation's work and funded projects led by another presenter (PR).

(2) talk about benefits
```
01    AT:          the conference has been muted.
02                 (2.2)
03    MO:  →       okay, I don't see >any other< questions so,
04                 (0.5)
```

05		I'm gonna (.) take a break for a few minutes
06		and turn it over to Michael to talk about
07		the benefits.
08	PR:	aright well <u>th</u>ank you Joanne,

As the moderator mutes the conference (line 01) to bring the previous question-answer sequence to a close, we observe a 2.2-second gap in line 02 before she announces to the audience *okay I don't see any other questions* (line 03). It is worth noting that this marked gap is a space where audience members can virtually raise their hands or type in questions, thus potentially starting a new question within the Q&A component of the webinar. As no visual evidence is present for these two types of bids for the floor, the moderator first describes what she sees on the screen before announcing her next action, that is, *I'm gonna take a break for a few minutes and turn it over ...* (lines 05–06), once again leaving a small space for audience members to self-select and ask questions or bid for the floor in line 04 with a 0.5-second pause. She then selects another presenter to initiate the next component of the webinar (lines 06–07). By narrating the visual—the lack of other questions on the screen—the moderator, therefore, accounts for her immanent closing of this Q&A component of the webinar.

In addition to providing a prospective account for closing down the Q&A component of a webinar, narrating the visual is also used to account for an upcoming sequence initiation. In the excerpt below, the moderator closes down the previous question-answer sequence by reading the audience member's understanding confirmation and appreciation, *got it thanks* (line 01); she then selects another participant to ask a question over the phone.

(3) another hand raised

01	MO:	→	(an' we're- he said) got it thanks, um te-
02		→	I see another hand raised now Teisha Cameron?
03			Teisha go ahead and hit star seven on your
04			phone?
05			(0.9)
06	AU:		actually you answered my question.=I'm
07			sorry. he[he thank you] very much.

After closing the previous sequence, the moderator narrates the visual by articulating that she sees *another hand raised* as well as announcing the hand raiser's full name (line 02), presumably what the applicant has used as their log-in name. Then, the moderator moves to select the participant with *Teisha* and *go ahead* and gives her instructions on how to make herself heard (lines 03–04). Importantly, in line 01, the moderator seems to have started reading Teisha's first name, presumably to select Teisha as next speaker, but cuts herself off at *te-* to first describe what she sees. The moderator thus accounts for her upcoming action of selecting Teisha as the next speaker by stating that she sees Teisha's hand raised on the screen.

At this point (i.e., after closing a question-answer sequence), it is worth noting that the moderator has two options: (1) to directly read the participant's name to nominate her or (2) to describe what she sees—the audience member's raised hand. The moderator's choice to describe the visual arguably demonstrates her orientation to her role in managing the interaction as not merely selecting the next speaker, but also informing the audience about how to be selected (i.e., the moderator will need to first notice a virtual hand raise before calling on the audience member). Given that the participants do not have the same level of visual access to what the moderator can see on her screen, nor do they have visual evidence of where on the screen the moderator is fixing her gaze, describing the visual fills in the information gap for the audience and serves as a way to virtually point the audience toward the next action that the moderator will conduct.

In these two cases, we observe that the webinar moderator deploys the practice of narrating the visual when transition to the next question-answer sequence or the next component of the webinar has become relevant. As we have shown, such a practice enables the moderator to provide an account to foreshadow and legitimize upcoming actions such as taking a break from the Q&A or nominating the next speaker, thereby playing a crucial role in keeping all participants "on the same page."

Providing a Retrospective Account

In addition to providing a prospective account, narrating the visual is also used to provide a retrospective account for a delay in completing an ongoing action—a delay caused by something that other participants might lack visual access to, be it something occurring within the webinar interface or in the moderator's physical environment. Extract 3 features such an instance, where the moderator is in the process of responding to a question that was asked earlier by a prospective applicant, but temporarily interrupts her own response to first describe what she sees on the screen—an already typed-in response to the same question from a colleague.

(4) drawing on their success

```
01   MO:           .HH <we had a question here earlier about
02                 (0.2) Health Project.=<in a community who
03                 had met the standards for Health Project. (0.2)
04                 .hh u:m. (.) <and was wondering about uh
05                 drawing on their successes there. (0.2) .hh
06                 a::nd u:::m (0.2) I would ju:::st (.) a:dd to- I-
07   →             I just see that (.) >$one of my< colleagues
08   →             answered tha:t question$ in writing to the
09   →             particular re- uh (0.2) °uh° (.) person
10   →             POsting the question. (0.2) .HH <but I just
11                 want to say we've had a nu:mber of
12                 applications in the pa:st?=who were working
13                 through the Health Project certification process?
```

At the start of the extract, the moderator provides the gist of an earlier question in lines 01–05. Rather than directly launch into the response, she pauses, takes an inbreath (line 05), and produces *and um I would just add to-* in line 06. The elongated *and um* followed by a short pause and the cutoff in the utterance *I would just add to-* seem to suggest that the moderator is heading toward framing her upcoming response as an addition to response(s) previously made available. This delay in responding is then accounted for by her subsequent narrating of the visual. As shown, she proceeds to offer a description of what she has visual access to, formulated as a just-made noticing of a colleague's written response to the original question asker (lines 07–10), introduced with *I just see*. Her own response is only resumed thereafter with an inbreath and a resumptive *but* in line 10 (see Choe and Reddington, this volume).

Note that this particular account for the delay allows the moderator to directly acknowledge a fellow representative's prior response that the audience should take into consideration, and in so doing, keep the different modalities of the interaction (spoken and visual; in-person and remote) and different participants (fellow representative, audience member who asked the question, and audience members at large) "in sync." For audience members seeking information related to their grant applications, this particular type of visual narration also enables them to connect and aggregate information received from both the visual and audial modalities and thus receive more comprehensive advice.

While the previous extract features the moderator accounting for a delay with a narration of the visual that connects responses across different modalities, the next extract shows a moment when the moderator uses this practice to account for a delay while she physically gets ready to initiate the Q&A component. Prior to this, she reiterated to the audience the available foundation representatives participating in the webinar as well as their contact information.

(5) get situated

```
01    MO:         .hh so we're gonna mo::ve to questions
02                no:w? (0.2) .hh a::nd um-
03                (0.5)-((quiet swallowing)) ts-
04    MO:  →      let me just take a moment to get re:situated
05         →      he:re? (.) .hh a::nd (0.2) our first question i::s,
06                what constitutes readiness to
07                apply:: for the award. (0.2) Elly? would
08                you: like (.) to comment on that?
09                (0.8)
10    PR:         .hh su:re,=Judy, u::m I'll start with some
11                general reflections,
```

As she finishes making a few final logistical announcements, the moderator moves to resume the main business of the webinar with *so* and announces that the presenters will be answering audience questions (lines 01–02). However, the Q&A component does not immediately start, and her multi-unit turn that transitions to and initiates the Q&A is temporarily halted; what follows is a micro-pause, elongated *and*, and a cutoff on *um* (line 02), as well as a slightly longer pause accompanied by a very quiet swallowing and lip-smacking sound (line 03). Such a delay, albeit very brief, is treated by the moderator as accountable, particularly in an interactive context in which the audience members only have visual access to what is currently being displayed on the screen—a Q&A placeholder slide showing information such as links to FAQs and a call for proposals. The moderator then accounts for the delay by verbalizing her need to *take a moment to get resituated here* (lines 04–05) before resuming the already-introduced action of taking audience questions (lines 05–06).

In this case, it is worth pointing out that narrating the visual as an account for a prior delay manifests further the moderator's orientation to what other participants cannot see and the need to remediate the unequal visual access. This is in part evidenced in the moderator's use of *here*, referencing her physical location in the account, which might indicate her orientation to the fact that other participants do not share her physical location and cannot see what may have led to the delay. We should also note that this extract features the only example in our dataset in which the formulation of *I + (don't) see/ be looking at + description of visual perception* is absent, since the moderator in this case is attending to her physical action which the audience cannot see. This suggests that the practice of "narrating the visual" is useful in making the unobservable "observable" and is not restricted to the description of one's own visual perception.

As shown above, narrating the visual can be used to retrospectively provide an account for a delay in the interaction, thus signaling to the audience members that the prior delay is not a cause for concern (as shown in Extract 5). The account can also entail helping the audience connect information made available in different modalities (as shown in Extract 4). In both cases, we observe the participants' orientation to treating visual phenomena as interactionally consequential.

Providing a Prospective and Retrospective Account

In addition to providing either a prospective or a retrospective account, we also observe that narrating the visual can help the moderator conduct both actions simultaneously. In Extract 6, the moderator describes what she is looking at on the screen to account for needing to "buy some time" before initiating the next question-answer sequence.

(6) whole communities
```
01    PR:           no.=I think you made um the points exactly,
02                  =Jenny, thank you.
03                  (1.5)
04    MO:    →      a::lright, I'm looking at >some of the<
05           →      other questions that are coming i:n?
06                  (2.5)
07    MO:           .hh u:::m,
08                  (2.0)
09    MO:           .HH (0.2) op-
10                  (2.5)
11    MO:           a:::lright. how about this one.
12                  how are who:le communities able to
13                  come together to tell their story of creating
14                  a healthy culture from multiple angles.
```

At the beginning of the extract, a presenter brings the previous question-answer sequence to a close with a positive assessment and appreciation for the response provided prior (omitted in the extract). A 1.5-second gap ensues (line 03), followed by the moderator initiating a somewhat delayed transition from this just-closed question-answer sequence in line 04 with an elongated *alright*. The subsequent narration of the visual (lines 04–05), where she verbalizes her in-progress activity of *looking at some of the other questions that are coming in*, thus retrospectively accounts for this delay in moving on to the next question. At the same time, it also offers a prospective account for the further delays in the form of gaps, inbreaths, perturbations, and vocalizations (lines 06–10) before the next question-answer sequence commences (line 11).

It is also interesting to note that the moderator narrates not a static image (e.g., *some of the other questions that we have*) but rather *some of the other questions that are coming in* (lines 04–05), using the present progressive tense. This suggests that her narration is responsive to the contingent nature of the interaction in this context in which applicants continuously type in questions that appear on the moderator's screen. As such, it also brings the audience who does not share the moderator's visual access up to speed on the question reading and selection process, through a kind of self-talk (Hall & Smotrova, 2013) that brings the backstage to the front for the audience.

Our final example occurs in a longer sequence during which the moderator and presenter attempt to invite audience participation, with little success. The moderator highlights a technological issue within the webinar interface that is hindering the overall progressivity of the webinar activities. Particularly, the moderator halts a request underway and then describes what she can no longer see on her screen to account for that request to the webinar operator (this webinar event is the only instance in our dataset in which an operator in charge of technological assistance participates).

(7) open up the phone line

```
01   MO:         .hh but I wonder if we can u::m (0.2) <Brian
02               I don't know how many people are on the
03               line?=and ope[ rator? ] can we ope::n- (0.2)
04   PR:                     [mhmm]
05   MO:  →      uh- >first of all< I'm not seeing who's on the
06        →      line anymore. u:::h [there was] a polling
07   PR:                             [ mhmm ]
08   MO:  →      thing and that took over.
09               (0.3)
10   MO:         .hh so can we see:: the participants,
11               (0.3)
12   MO:         who are <on> the li::ne? so (.) Brian could
13               u::m (0.2) maybe and Joanne could recognize
14               people?
15               (0.5)
16   MO:         a:::nd u:m (.) open up the phone line to
17               Everyone, perhaps.
```

In lines 01–03, the moderator starts to make two requests: *I wonder if we can* and *operator can we open-*, which presumably are directed at having the phone line open to all audience members so that they can start participating. However, both requests are cut off mid-TCU and abandoned as the moderator "steps back" with *first of all* to first narrate the visual in lines 05–06 and 08: She can no longer see *who's on the line* (the list of participants who are logged in) due to a poll that has occupied the visual space. Thus, the description of what she (no longer) has visual access to is used as a retrospective account for temporarily halting the request, signaling to other participants that she is experiencing a technical difficulty that needs to be resolved before she can complete the production of the request.

Then in line 10, with a resumptive *so*, she returns to the earlier course of action of making a request. She now formulates the request as *can we see the participants*, which is further elaborated on with the objective of enabling the presenter Brian and a previously identified audience member, Joanne, to recognize and nominate known participants to chime in (lines 12–14). Thus, narrating what the moderator no longer sees also provides a prospective account for redesigning the request as *can we see the participants* in order to enable two known participants to recognize and nominate audience members, which is a means for the moderator to resolve the issue of lack of audience participation.

Similar to previous extracts, narrating the visual enables the audience to be kept in the know while the "official business" of the webinar is temporarily halted. Additionally, narrating the visual serves as an immediate account for the request made to the webinar operator. By highlighting what she could no longer see (the participant list) and what she could (a poll activity that blocks her view), she makes relevant the operator's technological assistance and legitimizes her request that temporarily puts on hold the webinar agenda of inviting audience participation.

In sum, the above two cases show that narrating the visual can be deployed to both retrospectively and prospectively account for some kind of (potential) interactional trouble, such as a delay in implementing the next action or unsuccessful speaker nominations. With such narration, the moderators manage, again, to keep the audience members in the loop about the status of and ongoing activity within the webinar events.

Discussion and Conclusion

In this chapter, we have shown how moderators use the practice of "narrating the visual" to remediate participants' unequal visual access in webinar Q&A sessions by providing prospective and/or retrospective accounts. Narrating the visual may be used prospectively to account for and project an upcoming action such as the closing or initiating of a sequence. It can also be used retrospectively to account for a prior delay and signal to the audience that the event is still ongoing. Finally, narrating the visual can also be deployed to simultaneously account for a prior interactional issue and for an upcoming interactional project.

Although the participants in our data have very different levels of visual access to what transpires during the webinars (in terms of both what transpires in the room and on everyone's computer screen), *what* gets narrated is only what is treated by the participants as interactionally relevant, and this in turn becomes interactionally consequential: It shapes and facilitates the implementation of an ensuing action. By remediating the participants' lack of shared visual access, the moderator ensures that no one joining the webinar is left in the dark and "resyncs" participants' different levels of access to, and participation in, the webinar event. In other words, the moderator manages to keep everyone, interactionally, on the same page.

Our close analysis of this interactional practice in a specific kind of webinar environment reveals the following practical implications for those with the role of moderating webinars in professional settings. First of all, as evidenced in the extracts shown above, we recommend that moderators be equipped with a sensitivity to keeping the audience informed at every step during webinar events. Such sensitivity requires that, prior to a webinar event, the moderators fully assess what the webinar interface could look like to audience members, what they will or will not see, and what potential interactional trouble may occur. Since participants in face-to-face interaction and in webinar interaction rely on different sets of verbal, visual, and audial resources, it is advised that moderators preemptively address issues caused by different configurations of interactional resources and identify moments during which interactional trouble is more likely to occur. For instance, long pauses or gaps when changing speakers or transitioning to another activity are particularly accountable in the webinar context, given that the audience cannot visually search for an account themselves and may thus interpret silence as a sign of technical trouble; this could lead them to exit the webinar or make unnecessary, time-consuming inquiries to the moderators.

In addition to an in-depth understanding of the differences in interactional contexts and potential challenges, we also suggest that professionals tasked with moderating webinars be equipped with an interactional "repertoire" or "toolkit" of lines to deliver for specific situations. For example, when selecting and nominating an audience participant to speak, the formulation of *I see XX has raised their hand. XX please go ahead and hit star seven*, although seemingly rather mundane, can signal to other participants who is about to speak, issue a go-ahead to the nominated speaker, and provide specific instructions on how to participate for both the individual and the larger audience. Trouble could occur if any of the components is missing. Although it is difficult to predict all possible scenarios that one might encounter in a webinar, we believe a pre-packaged set of "useful remarks" at the ready could assist moderators in making smooth sequential transitions and help less experienced moderators gain a better understanding of how the webinar talk can be managed (see also King, this volume).

Finally, given the extra interactional work that results from the audience's lack of visual access, we would strongly recommend that organizations relying on webinars to communicate with external audiences preemptively resolve this issue by making available additional visual resources for participants (e.g., webcam feed of participants). Even if organizations might foresee issues related to limited bandwidth or a large number of audience members, it is still entirely possible to make available only the webcam feed of moderators and speakers, thereby eliminating some of the possibilities for the audience to be kept in the dark. We believe that, if equipped with an understanding of the specific features of the interactional setting, an interactional toolkit that preemptively addresses potential issues, as well as adequate technological support, moderators will be more prepared and successful in managing communication with the public in the webinar context.

Note

1 Preliminary analysis of Extracts 2, 3, and 6 appeared in Yu and Tadic (2018).

References

Garcia, A. C., & Baker Jacobs, J. (1999). The eyes of the beholder: Understanding the turn-taking system in quasi-synchronous computer-mediated communication. *Research on Language and Social Interaction, 32*(4), 337–367.

Goodwin, C. (2000). Practices of seeing visual analysis: An ethnomethodological approach. In T. van Leeuwen & C. Jewitt (Eds.), *Handbook of visual analysis* (pp. 157–182). London: Sage.

Goodwin, C., & Goodwin, M. H. (1996). Seeing as situated activity: Formulating planes. In Y. Engeström & D. Middleton (Eds.), *Cognition and communication at work* (pp. 61–95). Cambridge: Cambridge University Press.

Hall, J. K., & Smotrova, T. (2013). Teacher self-talk: Interactional resource for managing instruction and eliciting empathy. *Journal of pragmatics, 47*(1), 75–92.

Heath, C., & Luff, P. (1993). Disembodied conduct: Interactional asymmetries in video-mediated communication. In G. Button (Ed.), *Technology in working order: Studies of work, interaction, and technology* (pp. 35–54). London: Routledge.

Luff, P., Heath, C., Kuzuoka, H., Hindmarsh, J., Yamazaki, K., & Oyama, S. (2003). Fractured ecologies: Creating environments for collaboration. *Human-Computer Interaction, 18*(1), 51–84.

Maslamani, J. A. B. E. R. (2011). The use of silences/pauses in synchronous voice-based computer-mediated conversation: A conversation analysis perspective. *Newcastle Working Papers in Linguistics, 17,* 94–102.

Neyland, D., & Coopmans, C. (2014). Visual accountability. *The Sociological Review, 62*(1), 1–23.

Nishizaka, A. (2000). Seeing what one sees: Perception, emotion, and activity. *Mind, culture, and activity, 7*(1–2), 105–123.

Tudini, V., & Liddicoat, A. J. (2017). Computer-mediated communication and conversation analysis. In S. Thorne & S. May (Eds.), *Language, education and technology. Encyclopedia of language and education* (3rd ed.) (pp. 415–426). Cham: Springer.

Yu, D., & Tadic, N. (2018). Narrating the visual: Accounting for and projecting actions in webinar Q&As. *Studies in Applied Linguistics & TESOL, 18*(1), 31–35.

Part Four
Negotiating Identities

8

Constructing Expertise: Person Reference in Audience Members' Self-Identification in Public Talk Q&A Sessions

Ignasi Clemente
Hunter College, the City University of New York, and Louis Dundas Centre, Institute of Child Health, University College London

Introduction

Research on talk in institutional settings has examined how institutional asymmetries are enacted and identities negotiated (Benwell & Stokoe, 2006; Drew & Heritage, 1992). In this chapter, I analyze how practices for referring to persons, particularly initial self-references, are fundamental to how participants in the institutional context of public talks establish and enact the presentation of self, as well as how they position themselves *vis-à-vis* other participants.

A central aspect of the organization of talk is the selection of words to refer to objects, places, events, and people. However, there is no one-to-one direct relation between objects, places, events, and people and the label used to refer to them. For instance, a person called Ignasi Clemente can be referred to as *Ignasi, Ignasi Clemente, Dr. Clemente, Elena's son, my brother*, or *the professor who teaches at Hunter*. All these references are correct and applicable to refer to the author of this chapter. As Enfield (2013) succinctly puts it, "I cannot 'just label' the thing: There is no one way to label it" (p. 453). At the same time, because for a reference to be successful it needs to be shared by the speaker and their interlocutor, some of these references will be recognized by some people and not others. Thus, reference involves a choice among different options made for a specific audience in a specific context.

Person reference, mostly reference to non-present persons, has been studied in both ordinary and institutional talk (Enfield & Stivers, 2007). Conversation analytic studies, particularly Sacks and Schegloff (1979) and Schegloff (1996, 2007), identified two different preferences, minimization and recipient design, and several other practices that organize person reference. In terms of minimization, the preference is to use a single reference form/unit/package; in terms of recipient design, the preference is to use the reference that will be recognized by the recipient of the talk. The two preferences together can be summarized in the following maxim: use the simplest reference that will achieve recognition.

A second key distinction is found between initial and subsequent reference forms, and initial and subsequent positions. Initial reference (e.g., a personal name) occurs in initial position, that is, the first time a person is mentioned, whereas subsequent references (e.g., *she, he, they*) occur in positions that follow. Based on his examination of reference among co-present parties in telephone conversation openings, Schegloff (1979, 1996, 2007) highlights a third key distinction, between recognition and identification. In English, the vast majority of co-present reference involves the dedicated terms *I* and *you*, with *I* being the predominant form of self-reference. In openings of ordinary telephone conversations in past decades when no phone call identification technology was available, speakers calling family and friends recurrently expected that their voice would be enough for the call recipient to recognize who they were. When recognition was not achieved, callers used first names to identify themselves in the hope that it would be sufficient for the call recipient to recognize who they were. Recognition with just a token of one's voice by one's spouse, family, or friends was preferable to having to resort to identification.

As with other features found in ordinary conversation, person reference is specified and reduced in institutional settings (Drew & Heritage, 1992). In openings of telephone calls to emergency assistance centers, Whalen and Zimmerman (Whalen & Zimmerman, 1990; Zimmerman, 1992) have shown that callers do not expect to be recognized by call-takers, regularly do not self-identify, and remain anonymous. Call-takers use a categorical self-identification without personal names such as "Mid-City emergency" or "Nine one one emergency" to assure callers that their call has been placed to the center from which they are seeking assistance. Callers may use self-identification on certain occasions. Unlike ordinary phone calls where recognition is expected without self-identification (Schegloff, 1986), callers may use a first and last name that may be followed by location information. As they often lead to extended tellings, Zimmerman (1992) argues that a caller's self-identification is "hearable as a possibly prefatory element of the yet to be developed account of the call's business" (p. 450). Furthermore, callers may also use a categorical self-identification (e.g., "This is the Kit Cat Club"), in a parallel fashion with the categorical self-identification of the call-taker, which may also be followed by location information. With the categorical self-identification, callers establish themselves as institutional representatives of another organization without identifying who they are as individuals (e.g., providing a first and last name). A caller's categorical self-identification places the caller on a particular footing of "my organization to your organization," as well as in a special epistemological stance in terms of how the caller comes to have knowledge in an unmotivated and credible way about the trouble that they are reporting, and to have the knowledge to describe and categorize something as trouble (Whalen & Zimmerman 1990; Zimmerman 1992). Thus, a caller's categorical self-identification is connected to particular stocks of knowledge and rights to that knowledge.

In this chapter, I examine initial self-identification references in an institutional context involving public talks organized by a philanthropic foundation for audiences interested in health issues in the United States. In particular, I analyze how audience members self-identify during the openings of their questions for presenters and panel members.

Data

The findings that I present here are based on the openings of audience member questioning turns in Q&A sessions from fourteen public talks involving representatives of a U.S. philanthropic foundation. These were moderated public talks, with eight talks involving a single guest speaker and six talks involving guest speaker panels. In these public talks, panel and audience members vary widely, but both sets of participants include among them public and health policy makers, university professors and students, researchers, educators, practitioners, community activists, and CEOs of corporations and philanthropic foundations. Asymmetric access to conversational resources and to participation in the interaction between speakers on the stage and audiences sitting in front of it is clearly demarcated (Drew & Heritage, 1992; Heritage & Clayman, 2010). However, other omnirelevant asymmetries that are characteristic of institutional settings, particularly epistemological asymmetries in terms of differential distribution of knowledge and rights to know, are not delimited: The authoritative expert might be a member of the audience or of the panel. For instance, several speakers acknowledged explicitly during their presentations that they were reporting findings resulting from research conducted by prestigious researchers who were actually sitting in the audience.

Despite variation in the degree of formality, all the public talks follow a consistent pattern in which audience members limit their participation during the main part of the event to applause and laughter responses. After the main part of the event, audience members may talk during the Q&A session also in a highly regulated manner. Moderators are in charge of selecting and sanctioning which audience member will ask a question and whether the individual will have more than one opportunity to ask questions. In the case of public talks, the regulation of the access to the audience microphone imposes another layer of participation restriction. Audience members have to wait to be given access to the microphone, and the microphone may be taken away from them quickly after they ask a question. In most cases, audience members hand over the microphone as soon as they ask a question. At the same time, audience members exploit the orientation to the actual question itself as the official end of their questioning turn to talk extensively before posing a question (Reddington, Clemente, Waring, & Yu, forthcoming). As long as they do not ask a question, they can continue to talk and hold the floor.

Questions were identified according to formal and functional criteria (Enfield, Stivers, & Levinson, 2010). In total, sixty-five questions by sixty-four different audience members in fourteen public talks were identified. The question "proper" is perhaps the most salient component of audience members' complex and lengthy questioning turns, with questions often being very short and only formulated at the end. In these questioning turns we can distinguish sequentially and differentially organized components, including: greetings, self-identifications, gratitude and affiliative statements, question-qualifying statements (i.e., "This is an extensional question" or "Some related questions"), elaborate contextualizing prefaces in which audience members may provide background and/or reveal how they come to ask a specific question (Reddington et al., forthcoming), question announcements (i.e., "My question to you is" or "So the question is"), and the question "proper" itself. In terms of how audience members introduce themselves, most of the sixty-five questioning turns examined here begin with some form of self-identification: forty-three include the formulation of first and last name plus institutional affiliation, three include reduced self-identifications, and nineteen include none.

Analysis and Findings

In this section, I illustrate the recurrent practice of audience members referring to themselves by first and last name plus institutional affiliation (F&L name + affiliation hereafter) at the beginning of their questioning turns. I first describe the different components of this self-identification practice. Second, I analyze instances of what could be called deviant cases in which audience members self-identify partially, or produce some form of identification despite the fact that identification has already taken place. Following the conversation analysis research method of examining deviant cases as a way to "prove the rule" (Heritage & Stivers, 2013, p. 665), I argue that audience members may still orient to the expectation of an F&L name + affiliation self-identification while simultaneously being context-sensitive to other local and situated organizations and contingencies and to the minimization and recipient design preferences that organize reference in interaction. Thus, as Sidnell (2013) has observed: "As it turns out, deviant cases often provide the strongest evidence for the analysis because it is here that we see the participants' own orientations to the normative structures most clearly" (p. 80).

F&L Name Formulation + Affiliation

A first component of audience members' initial self-identification involves the use of a first and last name formulation, which is followed by a second component involving an institutional formulation, as, for instance, *Mary Stein from the Department of Health Science and Behavior*.[1] In Extract 1, the audience member (questioner hereafter) comes closer to the microphone, briefly greets the panel moderator/member, and identifies herself with an F&L name formulation that is followed by a single institutional affiliation with no mention of job title (e.g., chair, faculty, or director):

(1) Mary Stein
```
01    AU:    →    °hi there,° ((closer to microphone)) Mary
02           →    Stein from the Department of Health,=
03           →    Science=and Behavior=thanks for your
04                presentation. (0.2) .hh uh you've ↑mentio:ned
05                the U.K.::=and Canada::,=and >my
06                understanding< i::s that (0.2) .hh the
07                foundation ↑is doing ↑so::me global work to
08                maximize our learnings to:: >improve the
09                Framework for Health,< here in the
10           →    U↑.S., (0.2) .hh °can y↑ou talk about that?°
```

The questioner does not use a self-identification frame (Schegloff, 2007) such as *my name is*, *I'm*, or *This is*. Extract 1 is as compact as possible: simply F&L name without anything preceding it. Other self-identification forms in these data make use of frames. In Extract 2, the questioner first helps the moderator locate him, then uses the formulation *my name is* + F&L name and a brief affiliation and a gratitude expression that is also frequent in the openings of audience member question prefaces (Reddington et al., forthcoming).

(2) my name is Pedro Ruiz
```
01    AU:         <on the left.
02                (0.3)
03           →    um <my name is Pedro Ruiz,=<I'm with
04           →    The Health Initiative, (0.2) .hh u:m a:nd so:-
05                (0.2) .hh <I really appreciate u:m ((clears
06                throat)) a lot of u:m (0.2) >I mean< all of your
```

```
07                  <presentation.> (0.2) <and especially the
08                  power of data=<especially when it's put into
09                  ha:nds of community members, (0.2) .hh
10                  who can actually (.) be (.) a ↑pa:rtner (0.2)
11                  .hh <with a lot of the work w↑e're trying to do.
12                  <especially whe::n (0.2) .hh the i:ssues that ((continues))
```

In Extract 3, the questioner also begins her turn by helping the moderator/speaker locate her inside the large conference room, greets the speaker very briefly, and immediately follows with *I'm* + F&L name.

(3) I'm Sarah White
```
01   AU:         hi, [I'm on your: (.) right.
02   MO:             [((searching for the speaker))
03                   oh all I see is [(syl syl) ((hands up))]
04   AU:                             [ my left. heh heh    ]
05   →             hi I'm Sarah White with Children's Better
06   →             Care in Anycity Anystate. .hh an:d first of all I
07                 wanna thank everybody that's been involved
08                 in this, we're so excited with the release, we've
09                 ((continues))
```

Additional evidence of the strong orientation to an F&L name self-identification comes from instances in which even after the moderator identifies the questioner as doctor + last name or by first name only, the questioner nonetheless identifies herself with F&L name + institutional affiliation as shown in Extract 4 below. Notice that whereas the first identification contains the title *doctor*, is formal and deferential, and does not contain an affiliation, the audience member's second identification contains the nickname *Dan* instead of the full first name *Daniel*. In the next section, I reexamine this extract in light of the fact that while it clearly manifests participants' strong orientation to an F&L name self-identification, it can also be discussed as a deviation in regard to the more general organization of reference in interaction (Schegloff, 1979, 1996): There is a mismatch between reference form and position, as an initial person reference *form* (i.e., the audience member's use of his first and last name to refer to himself) is used in a subsequent reference *position*.

(4) my name is Dan Williams
```
01   MO:           ((moving to microphone))-thank you. u:m,
02                 I invite other people as you think of your
03                 questions to come up to the microphone
04                 a:nd we'll alternate microphones. so,
05                 Doctor ↑Williams.
06   AU:    →      °yes.° uh my name is Dan Williams, I'm in the
07          →      Department of Health Sciences. .hh uh (0.2)
08                 the vision you('ve) provided us is very
09                 ((continues))
```

These four excerpts show questioners' recurrent use of F&L name to refer to themselves as soon as they begin talking.

A second recurrent component of the initial self-identification reference is an affiliation formulation that names the organization at which questioners work or with which they are associated. The recurrent presence of an affiliation can also be seen in the four extracts shown above. In Extract 1, the questioner adds to the F&L name the formulation *from the Department of Health Science and Behavior*; *I'm with The Health Initiative* in Extract 2; *with Children's Better Care in Anycity Anystate* in Extract 3; and *I'm in the Department of Health Sciences* in Extract 4. These extracts illustrate some variability in terms of how the F&L name formulation connects with the affiliation, using prepositions such as *from*, *with*, and *in* (Extracts 1 and 3), and, in fewer cases, a full clause such as *I'm + from/with/in* (Extracts 2 and 4). In some cases, the preposition is also absent, resulting in F&L name + affiliation.

As is the case with F&L name formulations, institutional affiliation formulations display strong minimization and recipient design preferences. Minimization can be observed in several features of highly compact institutional affiliations, which recurrently contain only the name of an organization. First, most institutional affiliations do not include a position, title, or job description (e.g., chair, director, or CEO) that the self-identifying questioners occupy in that organization. Second, affiliations include a simple organizational reference (e.g., *Department of Health Science and Behavior* or *University of Arkansas, Little Rock* as opposed to a complex nested affiliation like *Department of Health Science and Behavior at the University of Arkansas in Little Rock*). Thus, affiliation is formulated as the name of an institution or an organization without reference to a larger organization to which the institution may belong (e.g., the department of health may be part of a university, hospital, or federal/state agency), or reference to a location (e.g., the city, state, and country in which the department of health may be located). Third, affiliation formulations include only one affiliation, despite the fact that questioners recurrently hold positions in multiple organizations. Some questioners do indeed name multiple organizations as they become relevant to points that they make in subsequent talk; nonetheless, they use only one when they first identify themselves. Finally, the preference for minimization can also be observed in the rare cases of an F&L name without an institutional affiliation: Questioners who are students/faculty of the university that hosts the public talk may add to their F&L name a descriptor such as *first-year grad student* or *faculty* without mentioning their university.

The selection of institutional affiliation reference also reflects the recipient design preference on multiple levels: Audience members orient to the heterogeneity of recipients that they have when asking a question, including presenters and panel members, the moderator, and the rest of the audience; to the specific point that the questioner is making; and to the specific amount of information that the questioner thinks their recipient needs to know: not too little, not too much, and, certainly, not information that the questioner believes the recipient already knows. In short, most questioners refer to themselves at the beginning of their questions with the formulation F&L name + institutional affiliation, and most self-identifications manifest a high degree of compactness and economy in both person reference and organizational reference.

Deviant Cases

In this section, I examine cases in which a component of the F&L name + affiliation formulation is absent or other components are added, as, for instance, *Hi I'm Max Cohen again*. I argue that these cases may nonetheless display an orientation to the expectation for this type of initial self-identification while at the same time, their deviation can be accounted for in terms of how reference is adjusted to specific situated contingencies according to the minimization and recipient design preferences that organize reference in interaction. In other words, the self-identification that an audience member will use for specific recipients in a specific context is locally managed and results from choosing among different options, as, for instance, the full F&L name + institutional affiliation, or a simpler reference that will achieve recognition. I have already mentioned one of these cases: the absence of affiliation in self-identification in questions by students and faculty who are part of the university that hosts the public talk.

A second set of cases is found in questions in which the individual asks a question for the first time but has already introduced themselves at a prior point during the public talk. In Extract 5, the questioner begins his questioning turn by greeting the panel member and producing an F&L name self-identification, which is not accompanied by an institutional affiliation. Instead, the questioner adds the adverb *again*.

(5) I'm Max Cohen again

```
01    AU:    →    hi:, >°I'm Max Cohen again,°< (0.2) u:m <so I'm
02                a researcher> I'm trained in research, and °I'm
03                trained in (.) looking at (.) uh a quality of data
04                (0.2) in r↑esearch >that (is) necessary< to make
05                public health or medical recommendation.°
06                a:nd uh researchers think (.) we have the
07                expertise in that, and researchers (.) and public
08                ((continues))
```

The prosodic delivery of the self-identification marks it as different from prior and subsequent talk. The questioner produces this F&L name self-identification in softer voice and in a rushed manner. He then pauses, initiates a word search, and slows down to provide a reference, a categorical descriptor (e.g., *I'm a researcher*) of a group of people that he belongs to, and that he considers relevant information to the project at hand, that is, to the question he is going to ask.

I want to make the argument that the combination of the distinct prosodic delivery of the questioner's F&L name self-identification and the use of the adverb *again* are related to the absence of an institutional affiliation. The questioner in Extract 5 faces a dilemma. He, like the audience members attending that particular public talk, was asked by the moderator to introduce himself and describe his work before panel members began their presentations and discussion. After the panel members finished, audience members asking questions during the Q&A session had to decide whether to self-identify for a second time, or assume that the panel members remembered who they were. In his analysis of "doing referring only," Schegloff (1996) has noted that initial references in initial position are personal names whereas pronouns such as *I*, *she*, and *he* are considered subsequent references because they are used in subsequent positions. Taking into account that audience members' introductions occurred at the beginning of the talk while the Q&A session occurred much later, should the beginning of an audience member's questioning turn be considered an initial position and contain an initial reference (i.e., personal name), or should it be considered a subsequent position and contain a subsequent reference (i.e., *I*)? With *I'm Max Cohen again*, the questioner in Extract 5 does neither. I argue that he displays an orientation to the recurrent F&L name + institutional affiliation self-identification at the beginning of a questioning turn while also displaying an orientation to the fact that audience members may recognize him with a simpler self-identification reference and do not need to be told again who he is. On the other hand, he does consider it necessary to remind panel members that he is asking such a question because of his experience and expertise as a trained researcher, a fundamental piece of background information for the question that he asks.

Other audience members asking questions in the same public talk and facing the same self-identification dilemma opt for different variations. A few minutes after Max Cohen asks his question, another audience member uses an initial reference in initial position at the beginning of her questioning turn, but it is not a F&L name + affiliation self-identification either. Instead, she refers to herself *as a person who lives in West Bay Beach and particularly deals with African American health.*

(6) as a person who lives in West Bay Beach
```
01    MO:         >°yeh.°< > we have a question in the audience?<
02                (0.5)
03    AU:         so m:y question i:s for all of the panel and it's from
04    →           uh (.) le:ns as a community-based organization as a
05    →           person who .h lives in West Bay Beach
06    →           and .h particularly deals with African American
07                health. .h we have tons of data. ((continues))
```

The questioner begins her turn with an announcement that the question is to be answered by any or all panel members (as opposed to a question for a specific panel member). This is followed by a question qualifying statement, *it's from uh lens as a community-based organization*, that explains the socioeconomic context from which the forthcoming question originates, typifies it as a particular kind of question that somebody who is experienced working with underserved populations would ask, and also impels panel members to interpret and answer it in a specific way (as opposed to understanding and answering it from the perspective of a public health official, a researcher, or an academic, for example).

Using the form of the third-person singular, the questioner's reference to herself is remarkable because it is not a first-person reference in initial position (*I'm Max Cohen*) or subsequent position (*I'm a resident of West Bay Beach*) but an initial categorical reference that describes a third party (i.e., someone who lives in West Bay Beach and deals with African American health).

Thus, the question is coming not from any community-based organizer, but from a community-based organizer who lives among that community in the specific neighborhood of West Bay Beach. Without self-identifying with F&L name + affiliation, as she did during audience members' introductions at the beginning of the public talk, she provides specific information about who she is while sparing panel members from being told again her name and the name of her organization. At the same time, it is significant that she does not use a subsequent reference *I* that would be consistent with an understanding that audience members already know who she is. Instead, she reintroduces herself with an initial description that identifies her as a category (i.e., a person who lives in West Bay Beach) and not as a particular individual, and which provides panel members with information that she considers that they need to know about herself in order to answer the question that she is about to ask.

A third set of cases that deviate from initial F&L name + affiliation self-identification is found in exchanges in which the moderator identifies the questioner with a name formulation and the audience member identifies themselves immediately after it. The deviance entails two *initial* person references back-to-back, the first one in initial position and produced by the moderator and the second one in a subsequent position produced by the audience member themselves. In most cases, moderators in the present data do not refer to and address questioners by name as they select them to ask a question. However, moderators on seven occasions use either the first name of the questioner, or, alternatively, a title + last name formulation, *doctor* being the most common title used as these public talks are health-focused. For instance, the questioner is referred to by the moderator as *Doctor Williams* in Extract 4 above. As noted earlier, while cases such as Extract 4 illustrate the recurrence of F&L name + affiliation self-identification at the beginning of audience members' questioning turns, they can also be considered deviations in terms of Schegloff's (1979, 1996) description of the organization of reference in interaction; that is, initial reference *forms* are used in initial reference *positions*, and subsequent *forms* in *subsequent* positions. One could consider that the questioner does not need to self-identify at the beginning of their questioning turn, since the moderator has already identified them. However, questioners identify themselves again in four of these seven cases. These second identifications differ in all cases from the one used by the moderator: Questioners instead use an F&L name + affiliation, an initial reference in a position that is, referentially speaking, subsequent, since the questioner has already been identified. In Extract 4, after having been referred to by the moderator as *Doctor Williams*, the questioner goes on to identify himself with *my name is Dan Williams, I'm in the Department of Health Sciences*. Despite the fact it could be considered "not needed," Extract 4 illustrates participants' strong orientation to an F&L name + affiliation self-identification at the beginning of questioning turns.

As in Extracts 5 and 6, the questioner in Extract 4 faces a practical dilemma of choosing how to identify himself at the beginning of his questioning turn but following a previous identification. An initial reference (i.e., *Doctor Williams*) has been used in initial position by the moderator and not the questioner himself. The moderator uses the initial reference in initial position both to select the next audience member to ask a question and to display that he personally knows the audience member. Following the moderator's identification, should the questioner assume that he has already been identified and use the subsequent reference *I* to refer to himself even though he is starting his own question? Or should he treat the beginning of his question as requiring an initial reference (i.e., personal name) in an initial position? Although he has already been identified, he chooses to treat it as an initial position, but uses an initial reference that differs from the one used by the moderator. In brief, the questioner begins his turn with the canonical F&L name + affiliation self-identification in a position in which it could be argued that it is no longer needed. His institutional affiliation is the only piece of information that may be news to panel and audience members.

With different solutions, questioners in Extracts 4, 5, and 6 identify themselves in ways that avoid repeating how they have already identified themselves—or been identified—before. Each of the questioners provides an initial person reference at the beginning of their questioning turns, orienting to the expectation that audience members generally self-identify, and, more particularly, self-identify with an F&L name + institutional affiliation formulation, when they begin to ask panel members a question. At the same time, they display an orientation to the fact that identification has already taken place, and, therefore, a simpler or different self-identification may be better suited at this particular point when identification is expected. In none of the cases does the questioner repeat the name formulation used by the moderator to name them, displaying a locally managed, recipient-designed fine-tuning of self-identification.

Discussion and Conclusion

I have illustrated the recurrence of the F&L name + institutional affiliation self-identification in the openings of audience members' questioning turns in public talk Q&A sessions. Furthermore, I have shown how, in some of the cases in which an F&L name + institutional affiliation self-identification is reduced or absent, participants still display an orientation to this type of initial reference formulation, as well as to minimization and recipient design preferences that organize reference in interaction (Schegloff, 1979, 1996). Following Schegloff's distinctions between initial (i.e., a person's name) and subsequent references (i.e., a pronoun such as *I*) and initial (i.e., the first time a person is mentioned) and subsequent positions (i.e., the following times the person is referred to), I have examined different audience members' solutions to the dilemma of producing some type of self-identification at the beginning of their questioning turns despite the fact that it follows a previous identification.

Although the solutions are different, they all share in common that they do self-identification without repeating the previously used identification. To conclude, I contend that rather than simply using a subsequent reference such as *I* in what is to all effects a subsequent position, audience members strive to identify themselves nonetheless because this type of self-identification is key to the enactment of an institution, to their presentation of self as authoritative institutional expert, and to the project at hand of asking a question.

In line with previous conversation analytic work on self-referring practices, these findings illustrate how reference is key in the construction of institutional talk and, more broadly, in the enactment of institutions. Unlike the use of no self-identification or only first name identification in ordinary conversation phone call openings, Schegloff (2007) describes how the use of the F&L name + institutional affiliation self-identification (e.g., *This is Penny Rankin from Lincoln*) runs the risk of being heard as an official business phone call, even when that is not the case. To counter the "official business" potential hearing of that self-identification, Penny quickly latches on a second referring unit *I'm a friend of Pat's*. Thus, referring to oneself using the F&L name + institutional affiliation formulation is not only found in institutional contexts but can be heard as constituting and enacting those very institutions.

Furthermore, these findings also illustrate how key aspects of person reference organization found in ordinary conversation are also found in institutional settings, despite the specifications and restrictions of institutional talk (Drew & Heritage, 1992). I have highlighted numerous aspects of how the compact and economic F&L name + affiliation self-identification reflects both person reference minimization and recipient design (Schegloff, 1979, 1996). It may not be surprising, then, that institutional self-identification reveals "institutional recipient design," which varies according to the specific person the speaker is talking to and the specific demands of different institutions. In Whalen and Zimmerman's (Whalen & Zimmerman, 1990; Zimmerman, 1992) analysis of calls to emergency centers, for example, the extreme time pressure to send an ambulance, the police, or firefighters, combined with dispatchers' need to codify the information and type it into a computer to be transmitted to the specific unit that will be sent to the location, results in a highly reduced opening in which the important information is not the name of the caller but the location to which the unit needs to be sent, the type of emergency, the veracity of the information, and the caller's epistemological access. Most callers do not provide names, but some callers use a succinct categorical self-identification without a personal name (e.g., *This is the Kit Cat Club*) to present themselves not as onetime users of emergency services. Rather, they self-identify as organization representatives who are calling another organization, who are conducting an official business call, who have experience dealing with emergency centers, and who know how to provide the information that the caller-taker needs to dispatch the assistance expediently (Whalen & Zimmerman, 1990; Zimmerman, 1992). Compared to onetime callers, the epistemological asymmetries in terms of differential distribution of knowledge and rights to know between institutional callers and call-takers are significantly reduced.

In the institutional context of public talks, audience members' institutional affiliations establish them as institutional representatives. But the recurrent use of the first and last name formulation points to the fact that who they are as individual persons is also relevant to the project at hand of asking a question and contains information that the questioners deem necessary for the question recipient to interpret the question. In addition to their institutional identity, their own personal involvement and work provide epistemological evidence of how they come to know what they know—for example, their professional experience, their training—and how they come to ask the question that they ask. In other words, not everyone who works at a non-profit organization, at a community organization, at a hospital, or at a university has the same training, knowledge, and experience. In a sense, initial F&L name + affiliation accomplishes multiple actions in a highly effective manner: It identifies the person asking the question, it is deemed by the questioners as necessary for understanding the question, and it positions the questioner *vis-à-vis* the knowledge/expertise that one needs to ask that kind of question. These initial self-referring practices are a resource for audience members to establish themselves as both institutional representatives and experts with knowledge over a particular domain of experience. As such, they also claim to have "legitimate" experience and epistemic rights to having such knowledge.

The institution-enacting identification that audience members use, although crucially located at the beginning of their talk, is not the only resource for building the institutional identity of an expert. Elsewhere in our data, self-identification, together with other forms of lexical choice and the use of institutional *we* (Drew & Heritage, 1992; Drew & Sorjonen, 1997), can be observed in how the audience questioners establish themselves very quickly as having authoritative knowledge about the topic. Combining these different resources, audience members construct presentations of an institutional identity of someone who finds themselves only circumstantially, locally, and asymmetrically in the limited position of an audience member of a public talk who has restricted participation and access to conversational resources (Drew & Heritage, 1992). The panel member may be on stage while audience members are below it, but F&L name + institutional affiliation is central to creating a more balanced playing field between those above and below it in terms of institutional epistemological asymmetries relating to the differential distribution of knowledge and rights to know. With the use of F&L name + institutional affiliation self-identification, audience members lay the foundations upon which to engage with presenters and panel members in more symmetrical peer-to-peer (Boyd, 1998), or from "my organization to your organization" (Whalen & Zimmerman, 1990; Zimmerman, 1992), relationships. The process that an initial F&L name + institutional affiliation begins then continues throughout the sequentially and differentially organized components of questioning turns, particularly the elaborate contextualizing prefaces that provide background and/or reveal how questioners come to ask a specific question (Reddington et al., forthcoming; see also Clayman & Heritage, 2002). As such, questions become opportunities not only to request information, but also for displaying expertise and positioning the questioner as knowledgeable (Ford, 2010). F&L name + affiliation is a highly compact and economic way to begin presenting oneself as knowledgeable and experienced in multiple institutional events, such as public talks, political events, city hall meetings, expert panels, and a wide range of professional meetings, that include opportunities for those who are not the main speakers to ask questions.

Note

1 All personal names and affiliations have been changed to protect the privacy of participants.

References

Benwell, B., & Stokoe, E. (2006). *Discourse and identity*. Edinburgh: Edinburgh University Press.

Boyd, E. A. (1998). Bureaucratic authority in the "company of equals": The interactional management of medical peer review. *American Sociological Review*, 63(2), 200–224.

Clayman, S. E., & Heritage, J. (2002). *The news interview: Journalists and public figures on the air*. Cambridge: Cambridge University Press.

Drew, P., & Heritage, J. (Eds.). (1992). *Talk at work: Interaction in institutional settings*. Cambridge: Cambridge University Press.

Drew, P., & Sorjonen, M.-L. (1997). Institutional dialogue. In T. A. van Dijk (Ed.), *Discourse as social interaction: Discourse studies: A multidisciplinary introduction*, (Vol. 2). (pp. 92–118). Thousand Oaks, CA: Sage.

Enfield, N. J. (2013). Reference. In J. Sidnell & T. Stivers (Eds.), *The handbook of conversation analysis* (pp. 433–454). Oxford & New York: Wiley-Blackwell.

Enfield, N. J., & Stivers, T. (Eds.). (2007). *Person reference in interaction*. Cambridge: Cambridge University Press.

Enfield, N. J., Stivers, T., & Levinson, S. C. (2010). Question-response sequences in conversation across ten languages: An introduction. *Journal of Pragmatics*, 42(10), 2615–2619.

Ford, C. (2010). Questioning in meetings: Participation and positioning. In A. F. Freed & S. Ehrlich (Eds.), *"Why do you ask?" The function of questions in institutional discourse* (pp. 211–234). Oxford: Oxford University Press.

Heritage, J., & Clayman, S. E. (2010). *Talk in action: Interactions, identities, and institutions*. Malden, MA: Wiley-Blackwell.

Heritage, J., & Stivers, T. (2013). Conversation analysis and sociology. In J. Sidnell & T. Stivers (Eds.), *The handbook of conversation analysis* (pp. 659–673). Oxford & New York: Wiley-Blackwell.

Reddington, E., Clemente, I., Waring, H. Z., & Yu, D. (forthcoming). "Doing being collegial": Participants' positioning work in Q&A sessions. In C. Ilie (Ed.), *Questioning-answering practices across contexts and cultures*. Amsterdam: John Benjamins.

Sacks, H., & Schegloff, E. A. (1979). Two preferences in the organization of reference to persons and their interaction. In G. Psathas (Ed.), *Everyday language: Studies in ethnomethodology* (pp. 15–21). New York: Irvington Publishers.

Schegloff, E. A. (1979). Identification and recognition in telephone conversation openings. In G. Psathas (Ed.), *Everyday language: Studies in ethnomethodology* (pp. 23–78). New York: Irvington.

Schegloff, E. A. (1986). The routine as an achievement. *Human Studies, 9,* 111–151.

Schegloff, E. A. (1996). Some practices for referring to persons in talk-in-interaction: A partial sketch of a systematics. In B. Fox (Ed.), *Studies in anaphora* (pp. 437–485). Amsterdam: John Benjamins Publishing.

Schegloff, E. A. (2007). Conveying who you are: The presentation of self, strictly speaking. In N. J. Enfield & T. Stivers (Eds.), *Person reference in interaction* (pp. 123–148). Cambridge: Cambridge University Press.

Sidnell, J. (2013). Basic conversation analytic methods. In J. Sidnell & T. Stivers (Eds.), *The handbook of conversation analysis* (pp. 77–99). Oxford & New York: Wiley-Blackwell.

Whalen, M., & Zimmerman, D. H. (1990). Describing trouble: Practical epistemology in citizen calls to the police. *Language in Society, 19,* 465–492.

Zimmerman, D. H. (1992). The interactional organization of calls for emergency assistance. In P. Drew & J. Heritage (Eds.), *Talk at work* (pp. 418–469). Cambridge: Cambridge University Press.

9

Gaze as a Resource for Creating Coherence across Speakers during Moderated Panel Discussions

Christopher D. Van Booven
College of the Holy Cross

Introduction

Public support is crucial to the longevity of any philanthropic organization. And the cultivation of strong, sustained support requires that philanthropic organizations find ways to deliver clear and compelling messaging to the public about key initiatives. One way that philanthropic organizations build public awareness of their work is by communicating about their various initiatives through the interactional medium of moderated panel discussions (hereafter MPDs). In an MPD, representatives of a philanthropic organization—who serve as "panelists"—discuss their perspectives about the work of the organization in the presence of a live audience. This panel discussion is facilitated by an individual—the "moderator"—who specifies the broader theme(s) of the discussion and poses theme-relevant topics to be taken up by the panelists. How to manage the participation framework (Goffman, 1981) of such multiparty interaction has not been a focus of much scholarly attention in conversation analytic work on institutional talk. This chapter investigates how MPD panelists, by deploying a specific set of verbal and gestural resources, manage the contradictory tasks of sharing diverse perspectives as individual speakers while communicating a coherent, shared message about their philanthropic organization across all panelists.

As a medium for communication between a philanthropic organization and the public, the MPD interactional framework has noteworthy affordances and constraints. For other promotional media, such as radio or television advertisements and public service announcements, members of the public are not present during the act of communication. MPDs, by contrast, provide philanthropic organizations with a platform for engaging directly with the public. Relatedly, though their discussion during the MPD is broadly structured by a moderator, most of the panelists' individual turns-at-talk unfold spontaneously for the audience—and all talk is delivered in real time. In addition, the presence of multiple panelists both reinforces and enriches the discussion of the philanthropic organization by exposing the audience to a diverse range of voices and vantage points. In short, by more closely approximating the spatial, temporal, and turn-taking characteristics of multiparty, naturally occurring conversation, the MPD interactional framework may help to make the panelists' talk—and, by extension, the work of the philanthropic organization—feel more human and relatable than other unilateral forms of communication.

On the other hand, where advertisements and public service announcements are able to ensure clarity of messaging through fully scripted and edited content, the comparatively spontaneous and real-time delivery of the panelists' talk in the MPD framework may run counter to the organization's goal of transmitting a clear, coherent message to the audience. This tension between spontaneity and clarity of messaging is further compounded by the presence of multiple panelists. While enriching the panel discussion with designedly complementary perspectives as individual members, the panelists must also take care to ensure that their contributions cohere with a broader message that is being conveyed about the philanthropic organization as a whole.

In this chapter, I focus on one interactional method that panelists use to counteract this tension between sharing a unique individual perspective and communicating a unified organizational message. Broadly speaking, this method involves temporarily emphasizing the relevance of a co-panelist during the course of a turn at talk. By temporarily "spotlighting" a fellow panelist during a particular spate of talk, the speaker is able to signal that responsibility for the spotlighted content—though delivered by an individual—is shared among various members of the philanthropic organization. Drawing on video recordings of MPDs with physically present audiences, I describe this method as an example of "tacit embedded addressing" (Lerner, 1993) in which the panelists, by orienting to themselves as a multi-person collectivity or "association" (Lerner, 1993), are able to speak as individuals but *be heard* as an association—namely, as the philanthropic organization of which they are a member. In so doing, I argue, panelists are able to encourage a hearing of their talk as reflecting the collective work of the philanthropic organization rather than the isolated efforts of an individual member.

Data

The extracts presented in this chapter come from a collection of ten publicly available video recordings of MPDs involving one major U.S. philanthropic organization. In this section, I briefly discuss some key characteristics of the participants and the interactional framework that will be relevant for subsequent analyses of the focal phenomenon.

Participants

Every MPD in this dataset involves three categories of participants—(a) audience members; (b) moderators; and (c) panelists—each with its own set of interactional rights and responsibilities. The first category of participants—the audience members—plays a vital role in this interactional arrangement, as they represent the "public" whose awareness the philanthropic organization is expressly aiming to build. Two features of the audience member category are important to mention here. First, the audience members are co-present; they are seated directly in front of—and therefore visible to—the moderator and the panelists throughout the MPD. Second, during the majority of the MPD, audience members are not eligible for speakership. With the exception of a brief Q&A segment, audience members' participation in the interaction is limited to recipiency.

Each MPD also features one moderator, who is responsible for several routine tasks: providing an opening statement to explain the broader theme(s) of the discussion; introducing the individual panelists and describing their affiliation with the organization; and leading the discussion by posing theme-relevant topics and nominating either the full panel or specific panelist(s) to take up each topic. In addition, where MPDs include an audience Q&A segment, the moderator invites audience members to pose questions—either orally or in writing—to which the moderator then invites either the full panel or specific panelists to respond.

A final category of participants in this dataset are the panelists, who number between two and five in each MPD. All panelists identify as co-affiliates of the philanthropic organization; however, every panel includes both internal staff and external community partners. Where the moderator assumes responsibility for speaker and topic selection, the panelists are responsible for developing the topics posed by the moderator (or by the audience via the moderator). In other words, though the broader themes and particular topics of the MPD are determined by the moderator, the burden of communicating those themes and topics to the public is shouldered principally by the panelists.

Interactional Framework

Owing to the participants' differential rights and responsibilities, the interactional framework of the MPD has certain organizational characteristics that differ in important ways from that of ordinary conversation. Two such characteristics bear mentioning here. The first relates to differences in normative intended recipiency across ordinary and MPD interactional frameworks, and question-answer sequences offer a useful case-in-point. In ordinary conversation, when a participant asks a question, an answer by some other participant(s) is made conditionally relevant—and this answer turn is typically (and intuitively) directed to one intended recipient: the participant who asked the question.

In the MPD framework, on the other hand, a moderator produces a question, which makes relevant an answer by a panelist—but the intended recipient of this answer turn is not always as straightforward as in ordinary conversation. In answering questions during the MPD, the panelists provide information that is requested by the moderator, and they design their turns to be fitted to the grammatical formatting of the moderator's question (e.g., affirmation/negation in response to a yes/no question). In this sense, the moderator as questioner appears to be treated as the intended recipient of the question's answer much as in ordinary conversation. However, because it is deliberately configured as a medium of communication between an "institution" (i.e., the philanthropic organization) and "the public" (i.e., the audience), the MPD interactional framework normatively positions the co-present audience members as primary or co-intended recipients for answers to all questions that emerge during the MPD—even when these questions are delivered and authored by another party (i.e., the moderator). A similar interactional organization has also been documented in the context of broadcast news interviews, where often the interviewer's "questions are framed as being raised not— or not only—for the journalist's own benefit ... but on behalf of a larger collectivity such as the broadcast audience, the citizenry, or the populace more broadly conceived" (Clayman, 2007, p. 221). As a consequence, as will be shown, the panelists typically direct their gaze to either the moderator or the audience while responding to moderator-posed questions.

A second organizational feature that is important to underscore is the normative length of individual turns-at-talk in ordinary conversation versus MPD interactions. In ordinary conversation, transitions in speakership occur very frequently. Indeed, when a current speaker wishes to maintain the floor beyond a single turn-constructional unit (TCU), she cannot simply continue speaking—her co-participants must observably demonstrate a willingness to proceed as recipients of an extended turn-at-talk. Where such extended or multi-unit turns require extra interactional "work" in ordinary conversation (Jefferson, 1978; Sacks, Schegloff, & Jefferson, 1974; Schegloff, 1980), the MPD framework routinely grants individual panelists the opportunity to hold the floor for an extended period. In fact, when a moderator poses a topic or question, the vast majority of panelists' response turns are delivered as multi-unit turns. This is because the panelists' turns-at-talk—rather than being interactionally "earned," as in ordinary conversation—are pre-allocated by the moderator and are thus, in a sense, "protected." In other words, once a panelist has been granted the floor to take up a topic or question, they may often continue speaking indefinitely—until they independently elect to bring their turn to a close.

Analysis and Findings

As will be shown, panelists deploy a particular coordination of verbal and nonverbal behaviors to "spotlight"—or temporarily emphasize the special relevance of—one or more co-panelists while producing an individual turn at talk. At the core of this method is one nonverbal resource in particular—gaze; that is, where (or at whom) the panelists "point" their eyes while delivering a turn at talk. Sequentially, the method unfolds in three phases. First, the panelist initiates or continues a moderator-allocated turn at talk with her gaze directed to the moderator or the audience. Second, without interrupting the flow of talk, the panelist shifts her gaze from the moderator/audience to a fellow panelist and simultaneously delivers a small spate of talk—either a word or short phrase—with one or some combination of the following behaviors: (a) marked stress; (b) a pointing gesture; or (c) verbal content recycled from a prior turn of the gaze recipient. Finally, the panelist directs her gaze back to the moderator/audience after producing the word or phrase and either continues or completes her turn.

With respect to social action, spotlighting is, at most basic, a method for doing referring. However, unlike other methods of referring (e.g., verbal reference), the nonverbal delivery of spotlighting enables panelists to do referring while simultaneously performing a different action with their talk—in this case, responding to a moderator-posed question. Broadly speaking, I argue that these tacit embedded references offer panelists a resource for resolving some fundamental tensions imposed by the MPD interactional framework.

In the sections to follow, I will show how spotlighting is used to do two specific types of tacit embedded referring—(a) reference to co-panelists' prior talk and (b) reference to co-panelists' identities—while the speaker simultaneously produces a response to a moderator's question.

Referring to Co-panelists' Prior Talk

One recurrent way that panelists use spotlighting is to highlight a connection between what they are currently saying and something that a fellow panelist said at some earlier point during the MPD. By revisiting their co-panelists' prior talk, the speaking panelist is able to emphasize that certain ideas are important not just to one individual speaker but to the panel as a whole. In so doing, the panelist is able to, in effect, contribute to the discussion as an individual speaker while simultaneously reinforcing a set of key takeaways about the shared work of the philanthropic organization. In this section, I present an extract that illustrates how a panelist uses spotlighting to observably attribute an idea to something her co-panelist had said several minutes earlier—but without making any explicit verbal reference to the co-panelist. The extract is taken from an MPD featuring a live (physical and virtual) audience, an independent moderator, and two panelists who are co-affiliates of a major philanthropic organization. The first panelist (identified as PA1 in this set of extracts) is an internal representative of the organization; she serves as the organization's president and CEO. The second panelist (PA2), an external representative, is the CEO of a large food and beverage corporation that partners with the philanthropic organization to address various public health challenges. As with many MPDs, the topics and questions posed by the moderator all relate to a common theme—in this case, the obesity epidemic in the United States.

In Extract 1a, PA1, the internal representative, is midway through producing a response to a moderator-posed question about the role of education in helping the general public to make healthy food choices. Just prior to where Extract 1 begins, PA1 has asserted that certain actors in the private sector have made promising strides in public education, citing the example of restaurants in the fast-food industry that have begun to model healthy eating practices by substituting low-fat milk and fruit for soft drinks and desserts.

(1a) portion size

```
01    PA1:            ((gaze to MO)) .hh so there're bright spots that
02                    we can see that again, .hh not only: (0.3) uh
03                    help (.) shape what- (0.4) people dema:nd,
04                    and (.) the way that they see: .hh their (.)
05                    food choices (0.5) over a lifeti:me, .hh
06       →            ((gaze to PA2))-bu:t u::h (.) will help to: uh-
07       →            ((gaze to MO)) (1.0) {((points to PA2))-address}
08       →            those issues of what the right portion should be.
```

From lines 01 through 02, PA1 begins to articulate the main point of her anecdote about healthy options at fast-food restaurants by stating *so there're bright spots that we can see*. Then, from lines 02 through line 05, she continues to articulate this point by introducing a "not only" contrastive structure—*that again not only help shape what people demand and the way that they see their food choices over a lifetime*—that projects an immediately forthcoming "but X" clause. Indeed, from lines 06 through 08, PA1 produces the projected "but X" clause—*but will help to address those issues of what the right portion should be*—and brings her turn to completion.

If one were to restrict analysis of Extract 1a to the talk alone, PA1's turn would appear to be performing a single action—developing topic talk in response to a moderator-posed question. However, when taking into account PA1's nonverbal behaviors, the "but X" clause at line 06 appears to be doing more than developing topic talk; in this case, PA1 appears to be using the spotlighting method to embed a simultaneous secondary action of referring to her co-panelist's prior talk. Specifically, the data suggest that PA1 is tacitly attributing authorship of the idea of "portion control" to her co-panelist, PA2, who had first introduced the idea to the MPD during a turn-at-talk that took place 7 minutes earlier in response to a different moderator-posed question. The referenced turn-at-talk is provided in the following extract (1b), where PA2's original mention of the issue of portion control appears in lines 03 and 04.

```
(1b) portion size, initial reference
     01    PA2:         .hh how do you line up .hh the incentives for
     02                 nutrition and the incentives for agriculture. .hh
     03       →         the second, .hh ↑how do you address portion
     04       →         control.
     05                 (1.2)
     06    PA2:         .hh I think that's a big issue.
```

Returning to Extract 1a, PA1 exhibits several behaviors that suggest that she is making a retrospective reference from lines 06 through 08 to her co-panelist's earlier emphasis on portion control as an important issue. The first, and most striking, is a marked shift in gaze that occurs at line 06. From line 01 through the end of line 05, PA1 orients to the moderator (MO) as the intended recipient of her talk by keeping her gaze directed toward the moderator throughout. Then at line 06, PA1 shifts her gaze from the moderator to her co-panelist while initiating the "but X" clause, *but will help to address those issues of what the right portion should be.* Because PA1 visibly orients to the moderator as the primary intended recipient of her talk, a pronounced shift in gaze away from the moderator and toward PA2 appears as a marked behavior in this sequential environment.

A second piece of evidence that PA1 is performing a secondary referring action from lines 06 through 08 is the timing of her nonverbal behaviors; her gaze and a subsequent hand gesture toward PA2 are coordinated with the oral production of content recycled directly from PA2's prior talk in Extract 1b. At the beginning of line 06, at precisely the moment that she produces the conjunction (*but*) in the projected "but X" clause, PA1 shifts her gaze toward her co-panelist and maintains this gaze through the delivery of the incomplete verb phrase—*will help to.* Again, the timing of this gaze shift toward PA2 is not incidental; it is in this "but X" clause that PA1 revisits PA2's previously expressed concern about portion control. A subsequent speech perturbation (*uh-*) and 1-second pause at line 07 suggest a possible word search for a verb to complete the projected infinitive (i.e., *will help to X*), and during this time PA1 shifts her gaze back to the moderator. However, when PA1 does ultimately complete the infinitive phrase to resume the broader "but X" clause—*address those issues of what the right portion should be*—she produces the main verb of this predicate—*address*—while simultaneously pointing toward PA2.

Taken together, PA1's marked gaze shift and hand gesture toward PA2, coupled with precision timing with content recycled from her co-panelist's prior turn, suggest that PA1's "but X" clause is doing more than simply developing topic talk. Rather, PA1 appears to be simultaneously doing a kind of referring—in this case indexing her co-panelist's prior talk. By "spotlighting"— or visibly signaling the special relevance of her co-panelist during talk about *portion control*—the speaking panelist is able to attribute authorship of that particular spate of talk to her co-panelist.

An embedded nonverbal reference to a co-panelist's prior talk offers panelists a useful technique for managing the competing demands of contributing an individual perspective while communicating a consistent message across multiple speakers. In an interactional medium that is advertised as a "discussion," but where the majority of talk appears in the form of lengthy monologues, each turn-at-talk bears a risk of presenting an idiosyncratic rather than unified view of the philanthropic organization. As a consequence, every speaking panelist must undertake extra efforts to ensure that individual experiences are bound by a thread of common messaging across speakers. One concrete way to accomplish coherence across speakers is for panelists to simply revisit ideas that were previously discussed by another panelist. An idea that is taken up and emphasized as important by more than one panelist is likely to become more salient as a "key takeaway" for the panel as a whole.

What is noteworthy about spotlighting is that it enables panelists to signal for the audience when an idea is being revisited—and encourage its hearing as a key takeaway—but without interrupting the primary action of their ongoing turn. As noted in Extract 1a, PA1's talk alone appears to be delivered in the service of a single social action—providing a response to a moderator-posed question. However, by incorporating the gaze shift and hand gesture toward PA2 in lines 06 through 08, PA1 is able to seamlessly integrate a visible signal to the audience: "this 'but X' clause contains an idea that was previously emphasized as important by my co-panelist, and it is also important to me." In so doing, PA1 is able to encourage a hearing of *portion control* as a key takeaway for the panel as a whole while simultaneously offering an individual perspective about the role of public education in managing the obesity epidemic.

Referring to Co-panelists' Identities

In addition to referring to their co-panelists' prior talk, panelists also routinely use spotlighting to do a different kind of referring, which can be broadly understood as making a reference to their co-panelists' identities. In referring to their co-panelists' identities, a speaker may refer to identities that she either shares or does not share with the referred-to panelist. In this section, I present extracts that illustrate these two types of reference to a co-panelist's identity: (a) reference to an identity that is shared by the speaking panelist and the referee and (b) reference to an unshared identity. These extracts are taken from an MPD that featured one moderator, four panelists, and a live (physical and virtual) audience. In this MPD, the four panelists and the moderator were all collaborating members of FLASH,[1] an initiative of one major philanthropic organization that brings together experts from multiple industries to address three core issues: racial equity, health, and climate change. The thematic focus of this MPD was FLASH's interdisciplinary approach to address public health challenges, and the panel was therefore composed of expert members representing various fields, including health, finance, philanthropy, and community outreach.

While MPD panels are often deliberately composed of representatives from different fields, occasionally there is overlapping professional expertise among one or more panelists. In such cases, a speaking panelist may occasionally make relevant a shared professional identity with a co-panelist during the course of a turn-at-talk. For example, in Extract 2, a panelist, PA1, invokes her identity as a health professional while stressing the importance of avoiding an exclusive focus on outcomes in the area of health and community development.

(2) reference to shared identity, health professionals
```
01    PA1:   →       ((gaze to AU)) .hh and certainly (.) those of us
02           →       in the health wo[rld kno:w,] .hh three years
03    PA2:                           [(( nods )) ]
04    PA1:   →       isn't gonna=get u:s. ((gaze to PA2))-(1.0)
05                   ((gaze to AU)) much of a health outcome.
```

Having just taken a position against an outcomes-exclusive approach, PA1 extends her turn-at-talk in Extract 2 by making an appeal for this approach on the basis of her experiences as a health professional. She begins this appeal in lines 01 and 02, where she identifies herself as a health professional using the phrase *those of us in the health world*. Several features of this self-identification are worth emphasizing here. First, though speaking as an individual, PA1 selects a first-person pronoun that is plural; *us* is typically used to refer to more than one person—self plus one or more others. Second, by incorporating *in the health world* as a modifier, PA1 effectively limits the scope of this reference to herself plus individuals who identify as health professionals. Having narrowed the referent to self plus health professionals, PA1 goes on to ascribe an exclusive bit of knowledge to this particular group in lines 02 and 04–05—*three years isn't going to get us much of a health outcome*. In other words, in the context of healthcare, an intervention lasting only three years is unlikely to yield substantive outcomes among the target population.

At this point, with analysis focusing squarely on her verbal behaviors, PA1's talk in Extract 2 appears to be directed exclusively to one action: developing moderator-elicited topic talk. However, the visible coordination of PA1's talk with several nonverbal behaviors, taken together with certain contextual factors, suggests that PA1 is simultaneously performing a secondary action: referring to a co-panelist's professional identity. The most striking evidence of this secondary referring action is a gaze shift that appears at line 04. Immediately after repeating the first-person plural pronoun, *us*, PA1 shifts her gaze toward another panelist, PA2. This gaze toward PA2 is maintained throughout a 1-second pause, after which point PA1 directs her gaze back toward the audience and completes the TCU. Having otherwise kept her gaze directed toward the audience throughout her turn, PA1's shift in gaze toward PA2 emerges as a marked behavior in this sequential context.

Further evidence of a secondary referring action comes from a combination of PA1's timing and word selection along with relevant contextual information about the panelists. At this point in her turn, PA1 is actively invoking the identity of a health professional and ascribing special knowledge of short-term health outcomes as a kind of "category-bound" attribute to all those who share this identity (Schegloff, 2007). With that in mind, PA1's gaze to PA2 at this moment does not appear to be incidental; PA2 is the only other self-identified health professional on the panel. Recall, too, that PA1 used a plural, rather than a singular, first-person reference form, *us*. As a non-explicit plural reference form, the pronoun *us* can theoretically be used to refer to self plus multiple configurations of "other(s)" (e.g., self plus one co-present other; self plus one non-co-present other; self-plus multiple co-present others; self plus multiple non-co-present others, etc.). However, there is compelling evidence that PA2, at a minimum, figures among the "others" indexed by the pronoun *us*. The first piece of evidence has already been noted—PA1's marked gaze shift toward PA2 at line 04 occurs precisely after she repeats the pronoun *us*. Put simply, because PA1 makes a verbal reference to "us health professionals" and then immediately turns to make eye contact with the only other co-present health professional, the inference that PA1 intends for *us* to be heard as including PA2 seems well supported by the details of the transcript. Furthermore, there is evidence that PA2 himself understands PA1 to be engaging in a referring action that includes a reference to his professional identity. At line 03, PA2 begins nodding his head in recognitional overlap as PA1 produces the final word of her initial first-person plural reference, *those of us in the health world*.

Extract 2 provides a prototypical example of a case in which a speaking panelist uses the method of "spotlighting" to highlight a professional identity that is shared with a fellow co-panelist. But "spotlighting" can also be used to index a co-panelist's professional identity that is not shared by the speaker. In this final extract I present one such example. In Extract 3, a panelist, PA1, is midway through an extended, moderator-allocated turn-at-talk. PA1 is a self-identified medical professional, and, over the course of his extended turn, he makes an elaborate analogy in which he compares the healthcare field to the automobile industry. To set up this analogy, PA1 refers to a hypothetical scenario in which all citizens would be required to have a car to go to work. In this scenario, PA1 posits that perhaps the automobile industry should assume responsibility for subsidizing fuel costs for low-income community members who lack sufficient resources to afford gasoline but are nonetheless forced to comply with a requirement that results in considerable profits for the automobile industry.

(3) reference to unshared identity, economist
```
01    PA2:           ((gaze to AU)) some folks would sa:y the people
02                   who are responsible for gasoline are- (.) all
03                   those people in the auto industry. .hh (.) who
04                   are profiting, (0.4) .hh from sale of automobiles.
05                   (0.3) .hh but not subsidizing gasoline.
06                   (0.5)
07    PA2:   →       .hh it's not exa:ctly an {((directs gaze and points
08           →       to PA3))-externality argument, [ .hh   ]}=
09    PA3:                                          [((nods))]
10    PA2:           =but it is an interesting argument
11                   about equity and who o:wns equity.-((gaze to AU))
```

At line 07, after articulating a position that places responsibility for subsidizing gasoline on the automobile industry, PA2 produces the TCU, *it's not exactly an externality argument*. Though grammatically complete, PA2 delivers the TCU with continuing intonation (line 08), which projects that the turn is still in progress. Moreover, the contrastive structure "it's not X," coupled with marked stress on the word *externality*, also suggests that PA2 will continue in order to bring the turn to pragmatic completion. Indeed, after a brief inbreath, PA2 continues the turn from lines 10 through 11 by appending a conjoining clause—*but it is an interesting argument about equity and who owns equity*—that completes the projected contrast with *externality argument*.

Omitting nonverbal behaviors from the analysis, PA2's TCU at lines 07 and 08—*it's not exactly an externality argument*—appears to be performing one basic action: doing moderator-elicited topic talk. However, if we incorporate observable behaviors beyond the talk into the analysis, a secondary referring action comes into view. And in this case, as with Extract 2, the evidence suggests that PA2 is using the "spotlighting" method to embed a tacit reference to the professional identity of his co-panelist. However, unlike Extract 2, the indexed professional identity is only attributed to the referenced co-panelist—it is not shared by the speaking panelist.

As with Extract 2, PA2 treats the audience as the primary intended recipient, and does so by keeping his gaze fixed on the audience for the majority of his turn. At line 07, however, PA2 temporarily shifts his gaze and manually points toward another panelist, PA3—and he times these behaviors precisely with the production of the phrase *externality argument*. In order to understand what these nonverbal behaviors are doing in this particular place in the transcript, some additional contextual information is necessary. First, the word *externality* is extremely infrequent in lay lexicon; it is a specialized term used nearly exclusively in one field—economics—and it refers to "a side effect or consequence of an industrial or commercial activity that affects other parties without this being reflected in the cost of the goods or services involved" (Externality [Def 1], 2019). It follows, then, that individuals with training in economics are much more likely to be familiar with the meaning of *externality* than those without such a professional background. Incidentally, PA3 is the only self-identified economist on the panel; approximately 20 minutes prior to PA2's turn-at-talk, he explicitly identified himself as such, saying, *I'm an economist, so I tend to think about things we can measure*. Finally, neither the term nor the general idea of *externality* appeared at any earlier point during the MPD, so, unlike Extract 1, PA2 does not appear to be making a reference to a co-panelist's prior talk.

In short, PA2 appears to be using the method of "spotlighting" to draw a visible connection between his use of economic jargon and his co-panelist's identity as an economist. In precise coordination with the phrase *externality argument*, PA2 executes a marked gaze shift and points toward PA3—the only self-identified economist present. What's more, PA3 observably demonstrates an understanding that his identity has been made relevant by PA2. At line 09, immediately after PA2 produces the phrase *externality argument*, and the accompanying nonverbal behaviors, PA3 nods his head affirmatively. The method of "spotlighting" is deployed in Extracts 2 and 3 to perform the same essential action—making a tacit embedded reference to a co-panelist's identity. However, what distinguishes the two extracts is the speaking panelist's own connection with the professional identity that is made relevant. In Extract 2, the speaking panelist makes relevant a professional identity that she shares with the referenced co-panelist—both PA1 and PA2 self-identify as health professionals. In Extract 3, on the other hand, the speaking panelist makes relevant a professional identity that he does not share with the referenced co-panelist; PA2 identifies as a health professional and the identity of economist is attributed exclusively to PA3.

Faced with the competing tasks of sharing a unique perspective while conveying a unified organizational message, spotlighting here presents a solution for contributing to the MPD as a more-than-individual speaker. Much like the embedded reference to a co-panelist's prior talk in Extract 1, the panelists in Extracts 2 and 3 counteracted the inherent monologue-as-discussion tension of the MPD framework by visibly implicating a fellow panelist as co-responsible for a particular spate of talk. However, where reference to prior talk promoted coherent messaging through a repetition of shared ideas in Extract 1, the embedded references to identity in Extracts 2 and 3 allowed the speaking panelists to bring their co-panelists' professional expertise to bear on their claims about key issues in the work of the philanthropic organization. By calling the audience's attention to—and pursuing tacit corroboration from—a co-panelist with a shared professional identity, the speaking panelist in Extract 2 was able to signal that her claim generalized beyond her individual experience to the healthcare field more broadly. And in Extract 3, where the panelist invoked his co-panelist's unshared identity as an economist, spotlighting enabled the speaking panelist to signal to the audience that his perspective—though filtered through the lens of a health professional—had theoretical support from experts in other disciplines.

In sum, by observably associating a particular spate of talk with the prior talk or identities of some fellow panelist(s), the speaking panelists were able to signal to the audience that the spotlighted talk, though delivered by a single panelist, was authored by multiple panelists. Said differently, the spotlighter communicates to the audience, "hear this as *my* talk, but *our* voice." Because the speaker is both physically and metaphorically indexing (i.e., "pointing to") some attribute of their co-panelist(s), this method can be broadly understood as doing referring. However, where other methods of reference are typically accomplished verbally (e.g., stating a person's name), spotlighting achieves reference using nonverbal behaviors—gaze, principally. What's more, when spotlighting occurs, the referring behaviors always constitute a secondary action in the context of the ongoing turn. If a speaker's primary action is, for example, producing a response to a moderator's question, the secondary action of referring to her co-panelist's talk or identity via spotlighting is seamlessly and "tacitly embedded" (Lerner, 1993) into the turn such that the primary action of responding to the question is uninterrupted.

Discussion and Conclusion

When communicating with the public through the medium of a moderated panel discussion, representatives of philanthropic organizations confront a fundamental tension—how can they speak about the organization as individuals with unique personal and professional perspectives while simultaneously ensuring that the audience receives a coherent message? This chapter closely examined one technique that panelists routinely employ to manage this tension: "spotlighting." At its most basic, "spotlighting" is a method in which a speaking panelist uses gaze to temporarily emphasize the special relevance of a co-panelist during a particular spate of talk. As such, "spotlighting" is, broadly speaking, a method for doing referring. In this chapter, the panelists used the method to accomplish two different types of referring: (a) reference to a co-panelist's prior talk and (b) reference to a co-panelist's professional identity. Though different aspects of the co-panelists' contributions and identities were referenced in each of the extracts presented, the method of "spotlighting" exhibited a number of defining characteristics that were common across all extracts. In every instance of "spotlighting," the referring action was always:

- accomplished as a secondary action in the context of the turn;
- "tacitly embedded" in the ongoing turn (Lerner, 1993) using nonverbal resources (i.e., gaze, principally) rather than talk; and,
- observably treated as a referring action by the speaking panelist (and, in Extracts 2 and 3, by the referenced co-panelist).

This chapter has provided evidence that "spotlighting" may serve as a useful technique for promoting coherence across panelists during a moderated panel discussion. Paradoxically, though framed as a "discussion," the vast majority of talk produced during the MPD takes the form of extended turns-at-talk that are, in essence, *monologues*. This is because, unlike ordinary conversation, most of the participants' turns-at-talk in an MPD are pre-allocated by a moderator. And once the moderator has granted the floor to a panelist, the panelist may typically continue as current speaker indefinitely—until the panelist independently opts to bring her turn to a close. These protracted, monological turns-at-talk not only place high processing demands on the audience, but they may also reinforce a perception of the speaking panelist as an isolated individual rather than an integral member of a collaborative philanthropic enterprise.

In all three extracts presented in this chapter, spotlighting offered the panelists a resource for managing the tension between sharing an individual perspective while communicating a consistent message across multiple speakers. In Extract 1, where "spotlighting" was used to refer to a co-panelist's prior talk, the speaking panelist was able to promote a shared message about the philanthropic organization by alerting the audience to themes that were common across the talk of multiple panelists. By revisiting and emphasizing the importance of certain ideas that were previously discussed by fellow panelists, the spotlighting panelist was able to make salient the specific ideas—such as "portion control"—that should be treated as "key takeaways" for the panel as a whole. In addition, when "spotlighting" was used to refer to a co-panelist's professional identity, the speaking panelists were able to demonstrate that their talk often generalized beyond their individual perspective by marshaling expert support for a range of positions. In Extract 2, for example, by indexing a shared professional identity, the speaking panelist was able to bolster a specific claim about the healthcare field by indicating that other health professionals—including the spotlighted co-panelist—could attest to the claim. And in Extract 3, by making reference to an unshared professional identity, the speaking panelist was able to reinforce the value of cross-disciplinary collaboration by demonstrating the value of borrowing and applying concepts (e.g., *externality*) from a field that is not one's own.

"Spotlighting" also presents other potential affordances that may enable speaking panelists to balance the interactional constraints imposed on them by the MPD participation framework. First, "spotlighting" generally allows the speaking panelist to break up the monotony of a single voice by inviting the audience to momentarily shift their attention away from the current speaker. To use the eponymous metaphor, by temporarily shining the "spotlight" on another participant, the speaking panelist is able to remind the audience of the eminently collaborative nature of the organization's work. And while the referring actions performed by spotlighting can also be achieved using the more common method of explicit verbal reference, the marked physical movements produced during spotlighting may also be advantageous because the audience is able to perceive these cross-panelist connections using multiple senses. That the audience is able to both hear and, in effect, *see* the act of connecting may help to make the connections themselves more salient and therefore more memorable. Finally, because the referring is achieved nonverbally and is always embedded as a secondary action in the turn, "spotlighting" may also prove to be more economical and less disruptive than alternative methods such as explicit verbal reference, whose oral delivery requires the speaker to temporarily suspend—and therefore delay—the primary ongoing action of the turn.

As philanthropic organizations make use of the moderated panel discussion as a medium for communicating with the public, it will be important to take careful inventory of the affordances and constraints of this unique interactional framework. By illuminating one potentially useful method that participants can use to promote coherent messaging across panelists, this chapter has underscored the central role of conversation analysis in developing such an inventory. And as this and other work on communicating with the public continue to develop, the case of "spotlighting" underscores the importance of attending not just to the things participants say, but to the things they do with their heads, hands, and bodies.

Note

1 Pseudonyms are used throughout to protect the identity of individuals and associations.

References

Clayman, S. E. (2007). Speaking on behalf of the public in broadcast news interviews. In E. Holt & R. Clift (Eds.), *Reporting talk: Reported speech in interaction* (pp. 221–243). Cambridge: Cambridge University Press.
Goffman, E. (1981). *Forms of talk*. Philadelphia: University of Pennsylvania Press.
Jefferson, G. (1978). Sequential aspects of storytelling in conversation. In J. Schenkein (Ed.), *Studies in the organization of conversational interaction* (pp. 219–248). New York: Academic Press.
Lerner, G. H. (1993). Collectivities in action: Establishing the relevance of conjoined participation in conversation. *Text, 13*(2), 213–246.
Oxford Dictionaries Online. (2019). Externality [Def 1]. Retrieved December 15, 2018 from https://en.oxforddictionaries.com/definition/us/externality.
Sacks, H., & Schegloff, E. A. (1979). Two preferences in the organization of reference to persons in conversation and their interaction. In G. Psathas (Ed.), *Everyday language: Studies in ethnomethodology* (pp. 15–22). New York: Irvington Publishers.
Sacks, H., Schegloff, E. A., & Jefferson, G. (1974). A simplest systematics for the organization of turn-taking for conversation. *Language, 50*, 696–735.
Schegloff, E. A. (1980). Preliminaries to preliminaries: "Can I ask you a question?" *Sociological Inquiry, 50*, 104–152.
Schegloff, E. A. (1996). Some practices for referring to persons in talk-in-interaction: A partial sketch of a systematics. In B. Fox (Ed.), *Studies in anaphora* (pp. 437–485). Amsterdam: John Benjamins.
Schegloff, E. A. (2007). Categories in action: Person-reference and membership categorization. *Discourse Studies, 9*(4), 433–461.

Notes on Contributors

Ann Tai Choe is a doctoral student in the Department of Second Language Studies at the University of Hawai'i at Mānoa. Her scholarly work has focused on conversation analysis and its applications to the study of multilingual interaction both inside and outside of the classroom setting, particularly focusing on epistemic management and emotions. Her recent research interests center around applying multimodal conversation analysis and membership categorization analysis to the study of service-learning interaction among multilingual speakers. Ann's work has appeared in the *Hacettepe University Journal of Education*, *Studies in Applied Linguistics & TESOL* (SALT), and the *Hawai'i Pacific University Working Paper Series*.

Ignasi Clemente is an anthropologist and a linguist. He is Assistant Professor at Hunter College, City University of New York, and Honorary Senior Research Associate at the Louis Dundas Centre for Children's Palliative Care, Institute of Child Health, University College London. His research interests include childhood studies; chronic and terminal illness; pain and suffering; health communication; and multimodality and corporeality in multilingual settings. He is the author of the book *Uncertain Futures: Communication and Culture in Childhood Cancer Treatment* (Wiley Blackwell, 2015), co-author of the book *Gestures We Live By: The Pragmatics of Emblematic Gestures* (De Gruyter Mouton, 2019), and co-editor of the volume *Discourses at the Edges of Life: Death, Communication, and Culture* (John Benjamins, forthcoming).

John Heritage is Distinguished Professor of Sociology at UCLA. His research focuses on social interaction and its interface with social institutions, with particular reference to medicine and mass communication. His publications include *Garfinkel and Ethnomethodology* (Polity Press, 1984); *Structures of Social Action* (co-edited with Max Atkinson, Cambridge University Press, 1984); *Talk at Work* (co-edited with Paul Drew, Cambridge University Press, 1992); *The News Interview: Journalists and Public Figures on the Air* (with

Steven Clayman, Cambridge University Press, 2002); *Communication in Medical Care* (co-edited with Douglas Maynard, Cambridge University Press, 2006); and *Talk in Action: Interactions, Identities, and Institutions* (with Steven Clayman, Wiley Blackwell, 2010).

Allie Hope King is a doctoral candidate in Applied Linguistics at Teachers College, Columbia University. Her current research focuses on classroom discourse, specifically what co-teacher interaction looks like through a conversation analytic lens. Her work has appeared in the *Hacettepe University Journal of Education* and *Studies in Applied Linguistics & TESOL* (SALT). In addition to her doctoral studies, she manages the Community Language Program, the lab school connected with the Applied Linguistics and TESOL Program at Teachers College.

Carol Hoi Yee Lo is a doctoral candidate in Applied Linguistics at Teachers College, Columbia University, and current president of *The Language and Social Interaction Working Group* (LANSI). Her research interests include pedagogical interaction, cross-cultural interaction, and the use of discourse markers in interaction. In particular, she pursues the question of how participants in the adult English as a Second Language (ESL) classroom manage understanding of the subject matter and understanding among themselves in her dissertation. She has taught ESL in various educational settings in Hong Kong and the United States. Her goal is to use conversation analysis as a tool to improve teaching and learning. Carol is a recipient of the Top Student Paper Award from the Language and Social Interaction Division of the National Communication Association (NCA), and her work has appeared in *Classroom Discourse* and *Studies in Applied Linguistics & TESOL* (SALT).

Elizabeth Reddington earned her doctorate in applied linguistics from Teachers College, Columbia University, where she is also an instructor. A past president of *The Language and Social Interaction Working Group* (LANSI), her interests include applying conversation analysis in the study of professional practice, particularly teaching. Her work, often in collaboration with other LANSI members, has appeared in journals such as *Classroom Discourse*, *Discourse & Communication*, *HUMOR: International Journal of Humor Research*, and *Linguistics and Education*.

Nadja Tadic is a doctoral candidate in applied linguistics at Teachers College, Columbia University, and editor of *Studies in Applied Linguistics & TESOL* (SALT). Nadja's research interests include classroom interaction and critical pedagogy, with a focus on identifying interactional patterns that can help increase marginalized students' participation, learning, and achievement. She has published work in *Language and Education*, *Linguistics and Education*, and *Studies in Applied Linguistics & TESOL* (SALT), and has presented research at conferences such as AAAL, IIEMCA, and IPrA.

Christopher D. Van Booven is an applied linguist with experience in language education and international programs administration. His research examines the development of adult second-language interactional competence in educational contexts that provide structured opportunities for naturally occurring conversation between native and non-native speakers, with a focus on study abroad in particular. He has taught courses in applied linguistics and Spanish at New York University, Hunter College, and the University of Massachusetts Dartmouth, and currently serves as Assistant Director of Study Abroad at the College of the Holy Cross. His work has appeared in the *NYS TESOL Journal*, the *International Journal of Science Education*, and the *American Educational Research Journal*.

Hansun Zhang Waring is Associate Professor of Linguistics and Education at Teachers College, Columbia University, and founder of *The Language and Social Interaction Working Group* (LANSI). Her recent books include *Theorizing Pedagogical Interaction: Insights from Conversation Analysis* (Routledge, 2016) and *Discourse Analysis: The Questions Discourse Analysts Ask and How They Answer Them* (Routledge, 2018). As an applied linguist and conversation analyst, Hansun's work has primarily been devoted to understanding pedagogical interaction, and, more recently, parent–child interaction and how institutional representatives communicate with the public. Her current book projects include *Storytelling in Multilingual Interaction: A Conversation Analytic Perspective* (with Jean Wong; Routledge) and *Micro-reflection on Classroom Communication: A FAB Framework* (with Sarah Creider; Equinox).

Di Yu is a doctoral candidate in Applied Linguistics at Teachers College, Columbia University. Her research interests include media discourse, political discourse, humor, and the use of multimodal resources in interaction. Di has presented at conferences such as IIEMCA, ICCA, AAAL, IPrA, and AILA. Her co-authored work has appeared in *Research on Children and Social Interaction*, *Discourse & Communication*, and *Language Learning Journal*. She served as president of *The Language and Social Interaction Working Group* (LANSI) from 2017 to 2019 and has also been serving as the web editor and book review editor for *Studies in Applied Linguistics & TESOL* (SALT). She currently holds a full-time administrative position and teaches undergraduate-level courses at Purchase College, State University of New York.

Index

address terms 121–4, 126
answers, *see* responses
asymmetry, interactional 5, 152
audience
    overhearing 6, 7, 9, 38, 39, 67, 88, 96, 100, 108
    positioning by interviewees 67–83
    questions 7–8, 91–6, 149–65

broadcast programming 6–7, 8, *see also* TV interviews

Clayman, S. E. 4, 6–7, 8, 9, 25–26, 43, 50, 173
collaborative completions 60–2, 63
computer-mediated interaction, *see* technology-mediated interaction
conditional relevance 14
conferences, *see* public talks
conversation analysis 4, 13
    methodology 13–15
    transcription conventions 11–12
courtroom interaction 5–6, 64

discourse markers 87–8
Drew, P. 64

everyday talk
    versus institutional talk 4, 6, 126, 150–1, 163–5, 172–3, 185
expertise, *see also* experts
    enacting 152, 164–5, 179–81
    referring to 179–84
experts 8–9, *see also* expertise
    interviews with 7, 8, 25–44, 49–65

first-pair part 14

Heritage, J. 4, 6–7, 8, 25–26, 37, 50, 57
Hutchby, I. 7

institutional talk
    features 5–9
    versus everyday talk 4, 6, 126, 150–1, 163–5, 172–3, 185
interviewer practices
    conveying neutrality 6–7, 25–6, 43, 64
    follow-up turns 49–65
    platform questions 25–44
    promoting foundation messaging 25–44, 49–65

gaze
    lack of in technology-mediated interaction 126, 131–2
    in panel discussions 169–87
gesture 174, 177–8, 182–4

journalist practices, *see* interviewer practices

Lerner, G. 62, 126, 171

messaging 4, 9
    by foundation representatives 67–83, 169–87
    interviewer role in promoting 25–44, 49–65
moderated panel discussions, *see* panel discussions
moderating
    panel discussions 96–8, 171–3
    webinars 99–100, 111–27, 131–44
Montgomery, M. 8

neutrality 6–7, 25–6, 43, 64–5
news interviews, *see* TV interviews

ordinary conversation, *see* everyday talk
overhearing audience, *see under* audience

Index

panel discussions 10, *see also* public talks
    audience questions 91–2, 94–6, 149–65
    moderator talk 96–8
    panelist talk 169–87
paralinguistic cues 118–20
person reference
    in audience talk 149–65
    in foundation representative talk 67–83, 179–84
podcast interviews 10
    interviewee talk 89–90
possible completion point 13–14
preference 14
    in person reference 150, 156–7, 162–3
public talks 10, *see also* panel discussions
    audience questions 92–4, 149–65

Q&A sessions
    in public talks and panel discussions 91–6, 149–65
    in webinars 99–100, 111–28, 131–44
questions
    animation 118–20, 125
    challenging 26, 28–9
    design
        in institutional interaction 5–8
        in Q&As 91–6, 149–65
        in TV interviews 25–44, 57–9, 105–7
        in webinars 114–20, 125
    platform 25–44
    prefaces 43, 50, 152–3, 154, 165
    preliminaries 115–18, 125
    wh- 32–36, 40–2
    yes/no 36–8

recipient design 150, 156–7, 162–3
referring
    to others 67–83, 150, 178–84
    to prior talk 174–8, 184
    to self 149–65
repair 14
reported speech 118, 119
reported text 118–20
respondent selection 121–4, 125–6

responses
    in institutional interaction 5–8
    interviewee 67–83
    interviewer 49–65
    resistance to questions 37, 105–7

Schegloff, E. A. 118, 150, 159, 161, 162, 163
Schiffrin, D. 88, 107
second-pair part 14
self-identification 149–65, 179–81
sequence 14
social categories 8–9, 67–83, 158–60, 179–81

technical difficulties, managing 97–100, 141–2
technology-mediated interaction versus face-to-face 126, 131–3
transition-relevance place 14
turn-constructional unit (TCU) 13–14
turn-taking
    pre-allocation of turns
        in interviews 50
        in panel discussions 173, 185
    speaker selection in webinars 121–4, 125–6
    turn allocation rules 14
TV interviews 10–11
    features 6–7, 8, 25–6, 49–50
    interviewee talk 67–83, 105–7
    interviewer talk 25–44, 49–65, 105–7
    types 7, 8, 26, 49–50, 64

webinars 10
    moderator talk 99–100, 111–27, 131–44
    recommendations for hosting 112–13, 127, 143–4
wh- questions, *see under* questions

yes/no questions, *see under* questions

Zimmerman, D. H. 150–1

www.ingramcontent.com/pod-product-compliance
Lightning Source LLC
Chambersburg PA
CBHW070637300426
44111CB00013B/2140